The Big Green Poetry Machine

Yorkshire & Lincolnshire

Edited by Annabel Cook

First published in Great Britain in 2009 by:

Young Writers
Remus House
Coltsfoot Drive
Peterborough
PE2 9JX
Telephone: 01733 890066
Website: www.youngwriters.co.uk

All Rights Reserved
Book Design by Spencer Hart & Tim Christian
© Copyright Contributors 2008
SB ISBN 978-1-84431-992-3

Foreword

Young Writers' Big Green Poetry Machine is a showcase for our nation's most brilliant young poets to share their thoughts, hopes and fears for the planet they call home.

Young Writers was established in 1991 to nurture creativity in our children and young adults, to give them an interest in poetry and an outlet to express themselves. Seeing their work in print will encourage them to keep writing as they grow, and become our poets of tomorrow.

Selecting the poems has been challenging and immensely rewarding. The effort and imagination invested by these young writers makes their poems a pleasure to enjoy reading time and time again.

Contents

Ackton Pastures Primary School, Castleford
Megan Marshall (9) 1
Nathan Whitehead (9) & George Steel (8)... 1
Courtney Roberts (9)............................... 2
Ellie Evans (8)... 2
Alex Barlow (9) 3
Georgia Pye (8) 3
Joshua Towler (9) 3

Clarendon Primary School, Great Lever
Khadija Musa (10) 4
Nasreen Atcha (11) 5
Zaid Seedat (10)...................................... 6
Zahra Bobat (9) 6
Husain Mohamed (10) 7
Lubna Atcha (10) 7
Abdullah Azam (10)................................. 8
Sumaiya Vali (10).................................... 8
Rumana Arif Ranguni (10) 9
Aysha Youssouf (10)................................ 9
Raheema Parvin-Hussain (11)................. 10
Samad Bilal (10)...................................... 10
Ibrahim Patel (9) 11

Eastfield Primary School, Immingham
Jessica Farr (10)....................................... 11
Tonicha Hiles (10) 12
Jamie Smith (10) 12
Melissa Ladlow (10) 13
Ashdon Love (10).................................... 13
Mathew Gollings (10).............................. 14
Victoria Barker (10).................................. 14
Georgia Horton (10) 15
Katie-Lea Bamford (10) 15
Tyler Holmes (7) 16
Kieran Pristley (10)................................... 16
Shannon Phillips (11)............................... 17
Anya Quickfall 8).................................... 17
Kirsty Wilson (10)..................................... 18
Sinead Kelly (10)..................................... 18
Elisha Best (10).. 19

Serena Glover (7) 19
Sophie Horton (7).................................... 19
Lewis Castle (7).. 20
Toby Tasker 20
Mathew Strugnell (10)............................. 20
Alana Russell-Rogers (7).......................... 21
Joe Cale (8) 21
Ryan May (7) 21
Kaven White (8) 22
Summer Fenwick (8)................................ 22
Bradley Ellis (8).. 22
Jacob Thornhill-Houghton (7) 23
Sophie Lane (8) 23
Chloe Gowing (7) 23
George Donner (10) 24
Joshua Rogers (10).................................. 24

Grange Farm Primary School, Leeds
Ela Trueman (7) 24
Chloe Spencer-Carter (7) 25
Eloise Morris (7) 25
Kieran Webster (7) 25
Conor Trainor (7) 26
Adam Varley (7) 26

Headlands Primary School, Haxby
Lydia Harrison (10)
   & Alex Richardson (11) 27
Emma Appleyard (10)............................. 28

John Harrison CE Primary School, Barrow Upon Humber
Stephanie Williams (11) 28
Hayley Potterton (11) 29
Natasha Spencer (10) 30
Jacob Evison (7)....................................... 30
Jake Mansfield (8)................................... 31
Chloe Catley (7) 31
Ami Binns (7) 32
Madison Horsfall (7) 32
Rachel Williams (10) 33
Reece Glew (10) 33
Shania Williams (8).................................. 34

Thomas Elam (10)	34
Natalie White (7)	35
Lucas Sinfield (7)	35
Fiona McLaren (8)	36
Abigail Standerline (8)	36
Mick Potter (10)	37
Jessica Brameld (10)	37
Charlotte Anderson (10)	38
Hannah Ward (10)	38
Bradley Campion (11)	39
Lauren Scott (11)	39
Lauren Higginson (10)	39
Michael Scafie (10)	40
Rebecca Millington (7)	40
Anya Portess (7)	40
Matthew Plastow (7)	41
Shaun Smith (10)	41
Cameron May (10)	41

Leeside Community Primary School, Heckmondwike

Kaleem Murphy (8)	42
Jamie Hanson (9)	42
Elliott Campbell (8)	43
Lauren Taylor (9)	43
Curtis Smith (9)	44
Molly Jones (9)	44
Malaiqa Ahmed (8)	44
Paris Taylor (8)	45
Rebecca Marples (8)	45
Ellie Adams (8)	45
Bethan Jones (9)	46
Ben Hardy (8)	46
Joseph Smith (8)	46

Manor Leas Junior School, Lincoln

Roisin Noonan (10)	47
Emily Elleray (10)	47
Crystal Wilson Clapham (9)	48
Katharine Dawson-Meadows (9)	48
Sasha Hate (9)	49
Hollie Jepson (9)	49
Greta Twine (9)	50
Aidan Stimson (8)	50
Lewis Smith (9)	51
James Waite (8)	51
Codie Paton (9)	52
Thomas Bontoft (9)	52
Sophie Armitage (9)	53
Chloe Bedson (9)	53
Hannah Newman (9)	54
Abby Wright (7)	54
Olivia Clinton (9)	55
Ebonie Evans (8)	55
Shianne Vanderhyden (8)	56
Lewis Dixon (9)	56
Megan Dexter (10)	57
Rhian Smith (10)	57
Ebony Wilson (9)	58
Abigail Tomlinson (9)	58
Clayton Evan (10)	59
Jack Forman (9)	59
Georgina Quarmby (9)	60
Kate Creasey (9)	60
Alice Twine (7)	61
Mia Horne (7)	61
Henry Jollands (7)	62
Harrison Wood (8)	62
Gemma Martin (8)	62
Jade Rodgerson (8)	63
Matthew McRobbie (7)	63
Jack Houlton (9)	63
Bethannie Cook (8)	64
Toby Evans (8)	64
Jessica Worrell (9)	65
Nathen Billard (9)	65
Elie Clark (9)	66
Aydan Christopher (9)	66
Eleni Papaioannou (8)	66
James Hobson (8)	67
Devon Chapman (10)	67
Macauley Webb (8)	67
George Flower (8)	68
Connor Price (9)	68
Matthew Flaherty (8)	68
Zach Peplinski (9)	69
Elisa Melina (8)	69
Finn Foster (8)	69
Jack Robinson (9)	70
Abbie Ellis (9)	70
Matthew Risebrow (7)	70
William French (8)	71
Charlie Turner (9)	71

Michael Nott (8) 71
Jasmine Greenhalgh (8) 72
Charlotte Parker (9) 72
Joshua Scrimshaw (7) 72
Lia Clark (8) 73
Liam Conlon-Bell (8) 73
Jake Goddard (8) 73
Chloe Lambert (7) 74
Ryan Hird (8) 74
Sophie Connell (9) 74
Kieron Price (7) 75
Khye Espin-Shaw (8) 75
Daniel Smith (7) 75
Benjamin Skinner (8) 76

Pollington-Balne CE Primary School, Nr Goole

Elizabeth Limbert (9) 76
Alex Austrums (10) 77
William Haggar (8) 77
Mae-Louise Hitchen (9) 78
Courtney Shaw (8) 78
Kieran Blackburn (8) 78
Peter Buckley (9) 79
Tadhg Keelan Parker-Walker (8) 79
Harry Free (8) 79
Maisie Louisa Nicholson (8) 80
Poppy Farrell (7) 80
Ben Kiddy (8) 80

Ryhill J&I & Nursery, Ryhill

Abbie Crossley (10) 81
Callum Burton (10) 81

St Paulinus RC Primary School, Dewsbury

Christine Agagon (10) 82
Bethany Whitelock (11) 82
Elizabeth Jennings (10) 83
Lauren Foxton (10) 83
Courtney Hewitt (10) 83
Fay Kilburn (10) 84
Madeleine Parkin (10) 84
Hannah Riordan (10) 84
Natalie Taylor (10) 85
Chloe Render (10) 85
Corey Blades (10) 85
Paris Bowler (10) 86

Joe Longstaff (10) 86
Liam Conway (10) 86
Bradley Hatfield (10) 86

St Wilfrid's Catholic Primary School, Sheffield

Ella Verity (10) 87
Oliver Fernandes (10) 87
Hannah Cowling (9) 88
William Quinn (7) 88
Tom Pathe & Alex Moone (10) 89
Matthew Dewhurst (9) 89
Catherine Pickin, Anna Wrench
 & Kate McKerrow (10) 90
Patrick O'Sullivan, Jack Shield,
 Euan McClafferty & Joe Curtis (10) 90
Nuala Pepper (9) 91
Amy Hughes (10) 91
Louisa Edwardson (7) 92
Madeleine Eddleston (10) 92
Louis Westoby (11)
 & Edmund Tooley (10) 93
Katherine Atkin (9) 93
Tom Hardwick (9) 94
Edward Blythe (10) 94
Liam Jackson (8) 95
Matt Cooper (9) 95
Eloise Brennan (9) 96
Luke Baldrey (8) 96
Gerry McDonagh (11) Carl Gillespie,
 Keiran Muter & Hakeem Ahmed (10) 97
Tullia Hinchliffe (10) 97
William Kidder (10) 98
Isabel Griffiths (11)
 & Francesca Gerrard (10) 98
Laurence Plunkett (8) 99
Phoebe Robertson (9) 99
Alfie Chester & Rory O'Sullivan (10) 100
Lucy Turner (10) 100
Peter Murch (8) 101
Isabella Breslin (8) 101
Hyunsu Doh (11) & Helen Alexander-
 Barnes (10) 102
Alice Sullivan (7) 102
Finlay James (8) 103
Daniel Mathews (9) 103
Lucy Gretton (8) 104

Claudia Llaca-Valeria (9) 104
Emily O'Brien (8) 105
Alice O'Brien (10) 105
Vivien Uttley (8) 106
Emily Catherine Parker (8) 106
Trishali Fernando (9) 107
Joey Humphreys (9) 107
Morgan Barrott 108
Joe Pepper (8) 108
Lydia McGuinness
 & Niamh Murphy (10) 109
Scarlett Jessop (7) 109
Chiara Natasha Hinchcliffe (10) 110
Aaron Robert Jessop (9) 110
Sam Gamblin (7) 111
Vinnie Kenny (7) 111
Cameron Bradley (11) 112
Eoin Doyle (9) 112
Rachel Dewhurst (8) 113
Amy Barnett (8) 113
Tom Brennan-Procter (9) 114
Archie Braddock (7) 114
Tom Eyre (8) 115
Joshua Fernandes (10) 115
Alexandra Davidson (8) 116
Will Speechley (8) 116
Francesca Danks (8) 117
William Allen (10) 117
Siobhan Phillips (7) 118
Matthew Quarrell (9) 118
Iona McKerrow (8) 118
William Gibson (7) 119
Matilda Alleway (7) 119
Zara Osako (7) 119
Hope Hogan (7) 120
Grace Woods (8) 120
Olivia Murphy (9) 120
Sam Keogh (10) 121
Sam Rodgers (8) 121
Isabelle Cain (9) 121
Hannah Simpson (9) 122
Dmitri Cheetham (7) 122
Rachel Mathews (7) 122
Alex Middleton (8) 123
Daniel O'Sullivan (8) 123
Francesca Shield (7) 123
Alex Yeardley (7) 124

Maeve O'Sullivan (8) 124
Mhairi Marciniak (10) 124
Benjamin Walsh (7) 125
Harry Curtis (8) 125
Hannah Sharples (7) 125
Loretta Deeney (7) 126
James Foletti (8) 126
Michael Smith (11) & Tom Uttley (10) 126
Bruce Gillespie (8) 127
Tim Pickin (7) 127

Sacred Heart Primary School, Middlesbrough

Shannon Lesley Byles (10) 127
Joeanna Appleby (9) 128
Samera Rashad 128
Chesley Conlin (10) 129
Declan Marron 129
Emily Craig 130
Bethany Hurst 130
Hannah Kay 131
Sophie Kendall (10) 131
Luke Henderson-Thynne (10) 131
Matthew Hughes (10) 132
Dell Labonete (10) 132
Georgia Gillespie 132
Paulius Sivecas (10) 133
Adam Loughran 133
Brad Gill 133
Sara Atfi (11) 134
Paige Graham 134

Wrawby St Mary's CE Primary School, Wrawby

James Harling (7) 134
Abigail Lucy Laycock (7) 135
Sadie Rickell (7) 135
Caitlin Almond (8) 136
Kizzie Platt (8) 136
Joshua Watson (7) 136
Samuel Lewis (8) 137
Steven Smith (8) 137
Edward White (7) 137
Charlie Reynolds 138
Tristan Miller (7) 138
Janey Smith (8) 138
Ross Tandon (7) 139
Nicole Barnard (9) 139

The Poems

Environment

Don't drop litter on the floor
Because it is bad for the Earth
And it is bad for the animals.
Don't drop paper, don't drop cans,
Don't drop bottles and don't drop plastic,
It can kill the Earth and the animals.
Put them in the bin.

Don't drop litter,
Don't drop bottles,
Don't drop cans,
Don't drop paper,
Don't drop plastic,
We are killing the Earth.

Megan Marshall (9)
Ackton Pastures Primary School, Castleford

Once Again

Don't use the car,
Use your feet.
Don't take the bus,
Use your bike.
Don't leave your TV
On standby.
Don't throw litter on the floor
Because you're killing
Me and you once again.

Nathan Whitehead (9) & George Steel (8)
Ackton Pastures Primary School, Castleford

Recycling

R educe, reuse, recycle and respect
E veryone needs to help
C arry paper to the bin
Y ou need to do your part
C oming soon, when I've put this in the bin
L ots of paper and glass on the floor
I n life we've got to be tidy
N ice and tidy
G reat to be tidy again.

Courtney Roberts (9)
Ackton Pastures Primary School, Castleford

Recycling

Recycle, recycle
Paper, glass and your cans.
Please remember the four Rs:
Reduce,
Reuse,
Repair,
Recycle,
To make the world a happier place!

Ellie Evans (8)
Ackton Pastures Primary School, Castleford

Recycle

R is for recycling
E is for the environment
C is for cycling to school
Y is for you to do your bit
C is for it is cool to recycle
L is for the litter that is killing the world
E is for everyone to help the planet.

Alex Barlow (9)
Ackton Pastures Primary School, Castleford

Recycling

Reduce, reuse, repair, recycle, respect,
Always remember recycling's the best.
Glass, bottles, paper, tins and cans,
Recycle them or they won't last.
Reduce, reuse, repair, recycle, respect,
Always remember recycling's the best.

Georgia Pye (8)
Ackton Pastures Primary School, Castleford

Poverty

No money,
No food,
Raggy clothes,
No house,
Very poor.
Poverty!

Joshua Towler (9)
Ackton Pastures Primary School, Castleford

The Great Green Outdoors

Can you not feel it?
That the Earth is shrinking?
It's all our fault
Because we are not thinking.

I have a dream
Of a great wide world,
Healthy and free,
Beautiful and green.

Of lovely wild flowers
Nodding with the breeze,
Of happy, content animals
Playing among the trees.

Of great wild cats,
Bounding and leaping
In their natural habitats,
While their cubs are sleeping.

Make sure the environment
Around you is chemical-free,
So the world is a better place
For all those to come,
And for you and for me.

Khadija Musa (10)
Clarendon Primary School, Great Lever

Life As We Know It!

It was a self-regulating system,
A newly-polished gem,
But life as we know it has
All changed since then.
Can't you feel it in the air,
The cry of the homeless birds?
Why does no one care?
The bare woods call me
With not a single tree,
The disaster has been made
By you and sadly, me.
Dear Mother Nature of
Man's pollution wasted
Water needs a lot of solution.
Wake up in the morning
And become a world-changer,
Like the signs of Mother Nature
Said before, the world is in code red.
Deep down in my heart
I can hear a voice of humanity.
I know you will help the ecosystem,
I give you a 100% guarantee.

Nasreen Atcha (11)
Clarendon Primary School, Great Lever

The Electric Environment

Switching on a light,
Listening to a CD,
Cooking a meal,
Uses energy.

There are the cities
With bright lights,
The electric's running
Although it's night.

Everyone thinks
Electric's free,
Everyone's got it
But not really.

Switch off a light
When it's night,
Save the energy,
Go eco-friendly.

Zaid Seedat (10)
Clarendon Primary School, Great Lever

Go For Green

Please don't throw rubbish on the floor,
Because if you do,
Listen to the clue:
Reduce, reuse, recycle.
Reduce all you can by
Turning off electricity.
Reuse all you can by
Making new models.
And recycle all you can by
Recycling paper and card,
Metal and tins, and plastic bags.

Zahra Bobat (9)
Clarendon Primary School, Great Lever

The Green Monster

Out comes the monster,
Searching for the right
To destroy living nature,
And is looking for a fight.

But we caused all this,
Look at the mess.
We need to work together
In this difficult quest.

He barges through the cities,
He barges through the green,
He's destroying everything,
He's very, very mean.

But it's too late,
The humans have lost,
We are all going to die
In 5 . . . 4 . . . 3 . . . 2 . . . 1 . . .

Husain Mohamed (10)
Clarendon Primary School, Great Lever

The Earth

This world would die without trees,
Don't cut them all down, please.
What will happen without shade?
These trees are not hand-made.

What's this pollution in the air?
That's absolutely not fair.
Stop factories from polluting the air
Get out of cars and start walking.

Lubna Atcha (10)
Clarendon Primary School, Great Lever

Going For Green

Our Earth,
It's our Earth.
Turn off lights
And walk to school.
Our Earth,
It's our Earth.

Close your taps
And do not drive.
Our Earth,
It's our Earth.

Recycle and
Save energy,
Save the ozone.
Our Earth,
It's our Earth,
Protect it!

Abdullah Azam (10)
Clarendon Primary School, Great Lever

Crazy Green Machine

The environment is important,
The environment is important,
We throw litter every day,
But never think about what they say.
Care for the environment!
Recycle, reuse, reduce every day,
Try at least once, think about what they say.
Care for the environment!
Plastic bags and hairsprays,
Deodorants and cans,
These are all CFCs.
Please care for the environment!

Sumaiya Vali (10)
Clarendon Primary School, Great Lever

Why Can't You Save All Species?

Environment should be clean,
All the plants should be green.
Our world should be chemical free,
This is better for you and me.

In the forest the trees have been cut down,
Now all the birds have a frown.
Make the world fun
With a shining sun.

Lovely flowers growing in the ground,
Can you not hear the love sound?
We should be thinking,
Not sinking.

Reduce, reuse, recycle,
And cycle, cycle, cycle!

Rumana Arif Ranguni (10)
Clarendon Primary School, Great Lever

Would It Be Good?

Would it be good if pollution was everywhere
And there were lots of bad gases in the air?
Would it be good if animals were not around,
Then there would be no animals found?

Would it be good if flowers were dull
And the world was not colourful?
Would it be good if Mother Nature was sad
And the world was very, very bad?

Would it be good if litter was always on the floor
And it was increasing more and more and more?
Would it be good if the sky went grey
And the world was polluted in every way?

Aysha Youssouf (10)
Clarendon Primary School, Great Lever

Endangered Polar Bears

Polar bears have been hunted
For thousands of years,
As a result of this,
The polar bears are nearly gone.

Global warming could also
Endanger polar bears,
By the warmness heating up the ice.
This means that females have trouble
Providing milk for the young cubs.

It is good that the government's
Created laws to protect the bears.
Who could destroy these beautiful animals?

Raheema Parvin-Hussain (11)
Clarendon Primary School, Great Lever

Mother Earth

The Earth is getting greater and greater,
So let's try and make the world safer.
If no one tries to make our world better,
Our world will be in danger.

Litter, litter on the floor,
Please recycle and help the poor.
Our future is in our hands,
Let's help and have a better land.

Pollution, pollution is everywhere,
On the road where cars are there.
If no one helps to make the world fair,
Then the world will become a nightmare.

Samad Bilal (10)
Clarendon Primary School, Great Lever

Don't Be Mean

Don't be mean, go for green,
Never give up,
There's always a chance.
Don't be mean, go for green.
Don't cause pollution
And find a solution.
Don't be mean, go for green.
Remember the three Rs, which are
Reduce, recycle, reuse.
Don't be mean, go for green.
Clean the Earth up
And don't mess it up.

Ibrahim Patel (9)
Clarendon Primary School, Great Lever

The Environment

Recycle all your rubbish
And don't throw it on the floor.
Think about where you put it
When you walk out of the door.
Litter-pick where you can
And look for a dustbin man.

Papers, chips and cans
Make our world an untidy land.
Scattered all around
We are duty bound
To make our world
Clean all around.

Protect our animals,
They are threatened.
We have a duty to protect
And our animals will respect.

Jessica Farr (10)
Eastfield Primary School, Immingham

Polar Bears

Why do polar bears have to die?
I know men aren't those kind of guys.
Do you think it's right to do
The things they do?

It's just so sad
And really bad.
I hear the cries at night,
Of the bears being slaughtered

Just to make rugs.
Polar bears are friendly,
They will give you nice big hugs.
They're pure white and black.

It's not just polar bears,
It's birds as well,
Disappearing over the years.
Polar bears are swell.

Tonicha Hiles (10)
Eastfield Primary School, Immingham

Extinction Poem

Tigers,
Now that people are hunting you down,
White tigers, you're safe now.
Owners are helping you one by one.
What about the elephants
That are hunted for tusks?

Golden eagle,
Eagles flying everywhere,
One of the fastest birds in the air.
Lots of species flying around,
Landing for prey on the ground.

Jamie Smith (10)
Eastfield Primary School, Immingham

The Endangered Tigers

Tigers today are getting extinct,
Why is this happening?
Please get this fixed.
Don't use their fur to make fluffy coats,
Just let them live,
And we won't have a problem.
Why do people kill anyway?
Is there a problem with tigers?
No, I didn't think so,
So leave them alone.
All they do is protect their babies,
But sometimes eat other animals.
Just think!
We eat other animals,
We protect our babies,
So is there a difference?

Melissa Ladlow (10)
Eastfield Primary School, Immingham

Little Bears

There they are, floating on the sea,
Trying to swim, but where can they be?
Round the corners and round the bends,
Still can't find them, that's the end.

Please help to stop global warming,
Help bears stay for another morning.
Bears are getting extinct because
You need to help to stop, stop, stop!

White fur with red drippings,
Ruby-red snow where he's laid,
Bleeding belly - what a shame,
What next? They'll all be gone.

Ashdon Love (10)
Eastfield Primary School, Immingham

Environment

How unfair,
People not treating others well,
Animals have died
Because of you.

Don't chuck litter
On the streets,
Put it in
Your pocket.

If you chuck litter
In the streets,
You will have
To pay a £1,000 fine
And you wouldn't like that.

Mathew Gollings (10)
Eastfield Primary School, Immingham

Polar Bears

Polar bears love you
As much as you do too.
Polar bears want to live on snow,
But why can't they live on it?

Polar bears love the snow
But are soaking in the water.
Polar bears love the snow and ice
But also skating on it twice.

Polar bears love to fight,
But fight with a load of snow.
We know they can't help it,
But why do they have to know?

Victoria Barker (10)
Eastfield Primary School, Immingham

Big Blue Whale

Whales swim about in the beautiful blue sea,
Whales dive down deep,
Far, far down.
Whales jump up high to breathe air.
Will that ever happen again?

How unfair, nobody's interested,
I don't find that good,
How about you?

Whales jump up high and spray water
Like a water fountain.
Whales flap their fins to swim.
Will that ever happen again?

Georgia Horton (10)
Eastfield Primary School, Immingham

Sadness To The Sea

Her body that leapt with joy,
With tricks we loved,
Happiness to the sea and the happiness she had.
She loved her daughter and she cherished her.
Why do you do this?
The laughter that surrounded her,
With smiles that surrounded her and
The cheers of the fans of her.
Bang!
The net caught her,
The sea filled with blood
And you see they're eating her now!

Katie-Lea Bamford (10)
Eastfield Primary School, Immingham

War

Who killed all the people?
Who are they, what are they going to do?
I'll tell you they're at war.
Who set the cannons?
Who drove the trucks?
Who fired the guns?
I'll tell you, the people.
Who cared for the kids?
Who kept the kids?
Who kept the kids in a shelter?
I'll tell you, they got adopted
Until the war ended.

Tyler Holmes (7)
Eastfield Primary School, Immingham

Care For Animals

How unfair!
No one has a little bit of care.
Animals need lots of really good care.

Do not cut down trees,
Even though we need the trees,
But if you do,
Plant three tree seeds.

Animals are becoming extinct
Just because we need it.
The future will go up
If you don't act up.

Kieran Pristley (10)
Eastfield Primary School, Immingham

Animals In Danger

Animals need help all around the world.
Humans are littering all around the world,
In ponds, trees, seas, everywhere,
So please stop littering today.

Animals dying all around the world,
Dolphins, monkeys, birds, chimpanzees,
So please stop littering today.

I can hear animals crying all around the world,
Lions, tigers, leopards, elephants, fish,
They're crying out for me,
So please stop littering today!

Shannon Phillips (11)
Eastfield Primary School, Immingham

War

Planes flying high in the sky,
Dropping their bombs from the sky.
The soldiers carrying their guns,
Not knowing what their day will become.
There is sadness all around,
Fear and death in the air.
Tanks patrolling the streets,
Searching and looking for the enemy.
We don't want the war,
We want peace and quiet.

Anya Quickfall 8)
Eastfield Primary School, Immingham

Extinct Foxes

It's not fair,
Foxes without care.
It's not nice,
Foxes without life.
Leave your rubbish,
You'll be punished.
It'll be killed
And you'll be billed
If you're bad,
You'll be sad.

Kirsty Wilson (10)
Eastfield Primary School, Immingham

Endangered Animals

I watch the dolphin dip in the sea,
I watch the elephant stomp to the beat,
I watch the giraffe eat the leaves,
I watch the frog jump for hours.

And I watch the seal getting cut.
How upsetting.

I watch the monkey swing from tree to tree,
I watch the worm squiggle about,
I watch the duck quack in the pond.

Sinead Kelly (10)
Eastfield Primary School, Immingham

Help The Animals Of The World

If you were a polar bear,
How would you feel?
If you were a pig,
How would you squeal?

Help the animals live life,
Save our creatures in this world!
Keep our planet clean and tidy,
Love each other as well as
Nature in our lives.

Elisha Best (10)
Eastfield Primary School, Immingham

Pollution

P etrol is spilling everywhere
O il fizzing, it's just not fair
L orries are going fast
L adies are dying everywhere
U gly oil tankers are evil
T raffic is long and I cannot get past
I nsects suffer and it will always last
O nly a few people care
N obody will be there.

Serena Glover (7)
Eastfield Primary School, Immingham

War

W hen will war stop?
A re we going to have peace?
R unning from the war.

Sophie Horton (7)
Eastfield Primary School, Immingham

Air Is Not Fair

P eople are dying of smoke
O il is just not fair
L ots of pollution is not a joke
L oads of gas is everywhere
U nable to breathe clear air
T raffic making dirty fumes
I t is not fair
O il killing animals
N obody cares about our world.

Lewis Castle (7)
Eastfield Primary School, Immingham

To Make The World A Better Place

P eople are dying of smoke
O il is fizzing, it's not fair
L ots of gas here and there
L oads of lorries make bad air
U gly creatures are dying each day
T rucks and vehicles are making bad fumes
I llness spreading all over the world
O nly we kids are aware
N othing will stop us, so beware!

Toby Tasker
Eastfield Primary School, Immingham

Save Us

Do you want us to live or die?
We're on the brink of extinction,
Do you care?
Soon we won't be here.

Mathew Strugnell (10)
Eastfield Primary School, Immingham

To Make Our World A Better Place

P eople don't care about our world
O il is causing the smoke to kill
L ots of factories produce lots of gas
L ots of smoke gathers on the hills
U nbelievable dirty, smoky clouds form in the sky
T rucks and vehicles are causing fumes
I llness is spreading deep down inside
O ceans are dying
N obody cares!

Alana Russell-Rogers (7)
Eastfield Primary School, Immingham

Pollution

P eople are not caring for the wonderful world
O il is spilling and causing trouble
L orries making smoke with oil inside
L oads of gas fizzing and people have died
U gly black clouds blocking the air
T hick petrol is everywhere
I llness while we speak
O xygen is very unique
N ever, ever spread pollution.

Joe Cale (8)
Eastfield Primary School, Immingham

War

W hen will war stop?
A re we going to have some peace?
R unning away from the army.

Ryan May (7)
Eastfield Primary School, Immingham

War

Who killed others?
What happened to the people?
Ill tell you, they were at war.
Who drove the tanks?
Who flew the aeroplanes?
I'll tell you, it was the soldiers.
Who looked after the children?
Who kept them warm?
I'll tell you, they got bombed.

Kaven White (8)
Eastfield Primary School, Immingham

Make Our World A Better Place

P etrol is spilling everywhere
O il is fizzing, it's just not fair
L orries are spitting diesel and petrol
L adies are sick everywhere
U p in the sky, dirty air, hard to breathe
T ons of smoke so beware
I mmingham docks are making smoke
O xygen is turning into dirty air
N obody cares about the world, *so beware!*

Summer Fenwick (8)
Eastfield Primary School, Immingham

War

W hen will the war stop?
A re we going to have peace?
R unning from the army now!

Bradley Ellis (8)
Eastfield Primary School, Immingham

War

We should not fight,
We should be friends.
Don't drop bombs.
The planes firing missiles,
The guns killing people,
There is danger everywhere,
The tanks scanning streets on the ground.
When will war end?

Jacob Thornhill-Houghton (7)
Eastfield Primary School, Immingham

Killing Animals

K illing animals is not fair
I gloos can melt
L ions scratch humans because they're mad
L iving creatures get mad
I gloos can't be eaten
N ever eat lions
G uns are hurting animals.

Sophie Lane (8)
Eastfield Primary School, Immingham

Killing Animals

Killing animals is not nice,
If you go and kill a woodlice,
Living things live everywhere,
Let them run around, be fair.
Goats are good, but don't kill them.
A bear is scary, but if you kill them
They will become extinct.

Chloe Gowing (7)
Eastfield Primary School, Immingham

Save The Animals

Animals are dying,
People killing without a care.
There is danger everywhere.
The world is cruel,
Humans think they rule.

George Donner (10)
Eastfield Primary School, Immingham

Environment

Why throw litter?
Why can't you put it in the bin?
Don't throw rubbish in gardens,
Don't wreck our environment,
Don't trash rubbish on the streets.

Joshua Rogers (10)
Eastfield Primary School, Immingham

The World Needs . . .

Recycle, not waste,
Love, not hate,
Peace, not wars,
Save the animals, do not kill them,
Walk, not drive,
Food, do not starve,
Bag for life, not a day,
Grow trees, don't cut them down,
To make it a better place.

Ela Trueman (7)
Grange Farm Primary School, Leeds

The World Needs . . .

Oxygen, not pollution,
In the bin, not on the ground,
Peace, not war.
Switch off, save electricity,
Walk, save petrol,
Turn off taps, save water.
Health, not sickness.
Grow trees, not cut them down,
To make it a better place.

Chloe Spencer-Carter (7)
Grange Farm Primary School, Leeds

The World Needs . . .

To be healthy, don't be sick,
Recycle, don't waste,
Turn off taps, do not waste water,
Love people, do not be mean,
Switch off lights, do not waste electricity,
Save animals, don't kill them,
To make it a better place!

Eloise Morris (7)
Grange Farm Primary School, Leeds

The World Needs . . .

Turn off taps, don't waste water,
Peace, not wars,
Food, not starving,
Cycle, no petrol,
Grow trees, don't chop them down,
To make it a better place.

Kieran Webster (7)
Grange Farm Primary School, Leeds

The World Needs ...

In the bins, not on the ground,
Peace, not war,
Love, not hatred,
Cycles, don't drive,
Food, not starvation,
Save the animals, don't kill them,
To make a better place.

Conor Trainor (7)
Grange Farm Primary School, Leeds

The World Needs ...

Trees, not stumps,
Fresh air, not pollution,
In the bins, no litter,
Peace, not war,
To make it a better place.

Adam Varley (7)
Grange Farm Primary School, Leeds

Tree Cutters

Rainforests we may never see
Are being cut down by you and me.
Insects are living in those trees,
Will they ever find their new house keys?
They're so upset they have to move,
They'll just have to get the new house groove.

If we had not done this now,
The queen of the wasps would sting you loud,
So tragically I have to say,
'Tree house cutters, you've got to pay!'
I look outside and I can see
Nothing at all, please help me!

If you can see I am a tree,
I am writing this poem for my mate, Lee!
Even though I am a branch
Without any pants!
I'll always see you cutting down me.

Stop killing our wildlife!

Lydia Harrison (10) & Alex Richardson (11)
Headlands Primary School, Haxby

Where Are All My Friends, I Wonder?

'Where are all my friends, I wonder?'
Said the polar bear,
'It's getting warmer, I don't need all this hair.'
And far across the other side of the world,
A monkey was hanging from a vine.
'Where are all my friends, I wonder?
The forest is getting smaller and we have lots more hot sunshine!'
And in another cold country a wolf was thinking,
'Where are all my friends, I wonder?
All the snow we have is melting,
And all the snow we usually have hasn't come!'
So let us think about those poor animals out there,
Who are losing their homes and friends.
You wouldn't like it, would you?
I wouldn't certainly, so please help me get the message through
To stop spoiling animals' homes.
It would make the world a better place for them and for you!

Emma Appleyard (10)
Headlands Primary School, Haxby

Being Homeless

I shuffle down the street like a snail
Leaving a trail of misery.
I drool as I look into shop windows,
Like a dog begging for a bone.
When I see any food on the floor
I dart like a bird for it to be in my hand.
When it is night I find somewhere to sleep,
Feeling afraid and unsafe.
When I wake up I do the same old thing,
Looking for food like a lost dog.
Would you like to be homeless?

Stephanie Williams (11)
John Harrison CE Primary School, Barrow Upon Humber

The Car Door Window

I sat in my car as it coughed up the road,
And I looked at the power station.
It was generating power for us again.
The black smoke rose like hungry vultures,
They looked me in the eye.

We coughed into the town, not too far away.
Plastic bags and empty Coke cans
Filled the street to the brim.
Some teenagers threw cigarettes on the ground,
Then the rain began to pound.

As we coughed onto the motorway,
The rain cried against my window,
Asking why it had to suffer,
Why, why, why?
I shrugged my shoulders sadly
And turned to face my mum.

We got to Nana's house, which was very clean.
I slumped into the armchair
Thinking about the things on our journey,
Then I stood up and thought next time
I would go back and clean, clean, *clean!*
Watch out, Pollution, I say what I mean!

Hayley Potterton (11)
John Harrison CE Primary School, Barrow Upon Humber

War

I sat up in my bed,
The war sirens went off and floated around my bedroom,
It was not yet destroyed.
I was in pain because I had no family,
I could hear cries in my closet!

In my toy box I heard whispers, they said, 'Help me'.
My bin had many noises: smashings, bomb droppings.
I was petrified.
Suddenly I felt someone grab my shoulder,
Oh it was like being suffocated.
I slowly turned around, it was only my duvet . . .

I shot downstairs and sheltered underground.
What if a grenade was here?
Bang! I saw a bomb drop on a house,
A little girl died with blood everywhere.
This is horror! Why is this happening?

Then I woke up with a sunny day, it was a dream . . .
But still this dream has happened,
Would you let it be like that again?

Natasha Spencer (10)
John Harrison CE Primary School, Barrow Upon Humber

War And Rubbish

Please recycle,
Don't throw stuff away.
Don't litter the street
And please tidy up
Because the world needs us.
Say no to war,
Don't kill other men
And say no to war.

Jacob Evison (7)
John Harrison CE Primary School, Barrow Upon Humber

Jungle Animals

In the big green jungle
Live lots of animals.
There are lots of animals
In the big green jungles.
In the jungle lots of animals
Are on four legs.
In the big green jungle
There are spotty animals
And also black animals.
The monkeys in the
Big green jungle
Are so chatty and funny.
The snakes in the
Big green jungle
Are so nosy and long.
The cheetahs in
The big green jungle
Are so fast.
In the big green jungle
All the animals are wild.

Jake Mansfield (8)
John Harrison CE Primary School, Barrow Upon Humber

Shine Up The World

The litter is bitter,
The world is a mess,
The litter bins are full
And they need to be done.
There is litter on the path, grass
And flying about on the road!
So we don't know where to go.
We need you to tell us
What to do first.

Chloe Catley (7)
John Harrison CE Primary School, Barrow Upon Humber

Untitled

If you have any litter,
Put it in the bin.
If you have any plastic or cardboard,
Put it in the recycling bin.
Don't put fags or litter
On the floors or roads.
Don't smoke indoors.
Save animals,
Earth is sad.
If you have any litter
Put it in the bin.
Pick up litter and
Put it in the bin.
Help injured animals.

Ami Binns (7)
John Harrison CE Primary School, Barrow Upon Humber

World War Poem

To make the world a better place
I know what I can do,
I can make a stop to war,
Because war is causing lots of problems.
It is really ruining the world,
The environment is dying
Because of this horrible thing.
It really isn't right,
War, it should die, it should be fought.
War is a hideous thing.
We fight and lose, but
Sometimes we win.
It's still a horrible thing.
Stop war!

Madison Horsfall (7)
John Harrison CE Primary School, Barrow Upon Humber

The Animal

I was as nervous as a rabbit
Wandering down the road.
I was as worried as a bird
Getting eaten.
I was running as quickly as a cheetah
Down the forest floor.
I darted to the grass
But the naughty fox was there.
I turned below freezing,
I zoomed to the bed,
I felt pain,
And fear.
You don't want this to happen.

Rachel Williams (10)
John Harrison CE Primary School, Barrow Upon Humber

War

War must feel like a gang on you,
Getting pulled apart like vultures eating prey.
Why can't it be like a gentleman's fight hundreds of years ago?

W ar is bad and very evil
A t war it makes everyone cry
R esources short and war is life-threatening

I hate war, myself
S ad, war is

B ut I had to fight in World War II
A mine left behind can kill innocent people
D ead, I am lucky not to be. Many are buried in the ground.

Reece Glew (10)
John Harrison CE Primary School, Barrow Upon Humber

Look After Everybody, Even The Animals

Look after your animals,
Care for your people,
Stop the wars.
Look out for your family,
Feed your animals,
Stop cutting down the forests,
Your animals must be safe inside.
We have to pick up the rubbish
And put it in the bin.
Look out for your animals
When they are lost.

Shania Williams (8)
John Harrison CE Primary School, Barrow Upon Humber

The Dangers Of War

The sounds are the horror,
The *zoom* is my fear,
The cries are my face,
The injured are my body
And the pain is my legs.

The death is my life,
The smash is my mouth,
The tanks are the ambush,
The sigh is the engine
And the deserted town is my school.

Thomas Elam (10)
John Harrison CE Primary School, Barrow Upon Humber

Flowers

Seed to flower, one week to grow,
First seed and water also.
Sun as bright as the moonlight.
In the morning, what a surprise!
A beautiful plant in your garden.
All different colours, yes, red, blue,
Orange, white, yellow and purple too.
Lots of shapes and sizes too.
Don't stand or leave anything bad around them.
Help make this a better planet for *you!*

Natalie White (7)
John Harrison CE Primary School, Barrow Upon Humber

Save The World From War

Please can you stop the war
Because children's daddies are
Going in to war and not coming back
Because they've died and
The children never see their daddies
Ever again.
So please can you stop the war
Because people are dying
And babies are crying?
So please can you stop the war?

Lucas Sinfield (7)
John Harrison CE Primary School, Barrow Upon Humber

Pollution

Turn off the TV,
Cancel computers,
Stop littering,
Don't make more landfills,
Turn lights off,
Is that all? No!
Rescue rainforests,
Stop war,
Recycle more.
Please help us!

Fiona McLaren (8)
John Harrison CE Primary School, Barrow Upon Humber

Animals And Rainforests

Rainforests are big and scary.
Rainforests are always muddy.
Animals are big and hairy.
Animals are always on the move.
Animals are always in the trees.
Animals are always on the loose.
Animals are always crawling round.
Animals are always lively.
Animals are sometimes clumsy.
Animals are always wriggly.

Abigail Standerline (8)
John Harrison CE Primary School, Barrow Upon Humber

As I Walk Down My Smoky Street

I cough, I splutter, I cry, I choke,
The sickening factories like huge cigarettes,
They make us fall to a smoky death.

I moan, I sneeze, I fall, I'm broke,
The sickening smoke, the dreary eyes,
The wheezy fumes are the Devil's demise.

The tears, the fears, the clutching of throats,
Another life gone, gone for all time.
Another life gone and they'll never be fine.

Mick Potter (10)
John Harrison CE Primary School, Barrow Upon Humber

Being Homeless

I get up with all my bags,
I put them on my hump,
I see more food, I drop my bags,
I run as fast as I can,
By the time I get there it has all gone.

I pick all my bags up,
I put them back on my hump,
I walk and walk,
I suspect I will get to that bus shelter tonight.

Jessica Brameld (10)
John Harrison CE Primary School, Barrow Upon Humber

Recycle Your Rubbish

The paper scurries like a rat,
Save the environment, recycle paper.

Cans are rattling in the streets
As rats and bats are trapped in cans.

Recycling bins are empty
As black bins are full.

So save the environment
Until recycling bins are full.

Charlotte Anderson (10)
John Harrison CE Primary School, Barrow Upon Humber

The Homeless Man

As he is cold, I am warm in bed.
As he is bored, I am having fun.
As he is lonely, I am with my friends and family.
As he is hungry, I am having a Sunday roast.
As he is unhappy, I am happy playing games.
As he is worried, I am joyful at home.
When it is Christmas he will be in a bus shelter,
When I'm at home, warm, opening my presents.
Would you like to be that man?

Hannah Ward (10)
John Harrison CE Primary School, Barrow Upon Humber

So Stop Now!

What is wrong with animals
Trying to find a home
Just like we do?
Why do you destroy animals' lives?
Would you like it if
Someone destroyed your life?
So just think about that,
So stop now!

Bradley Campion (11)
John Harrison CE Primary School, Barrow Upon Humber

The Rubbish Town

The rubbish is like a bird soaring through the sky,
The rubbish is like a butterfly flapping its wings,
For recycling rubbish can save an animal's life.
For every piece we recycle makes something new like an animal.
For every piece we drop makes a mess like moths' dust.
For when the bins are full they are emptied like chicken eggs.
Would you like to be a piece of rubbish floating in the sky?

Lauren Scott (11)
John Harrison CE Primary School, Barrow Upon Humber

Recycle

Should you put cans in the bushes?
Should you put glass bottles in rivers?
Should you put magazines in the middle of the road?
Should you chuck your paper on the pavement?
Should you chuck rubbish in the ponds and rivers?
It's just like killing an animal,
Please stop it.

Lauren Higginson (10)
John Harrison CE Primary School, Barrow Upon Humber

Being Homeless

Would you like to live on the street,
Without any food or drink,
And smell, so people call you names,
And live on the path?
All that you have is carrier bags
And you snatch things off people,
Would you like to live like that?

Michael Scafie (10)
John Harrison CE Primary School, Barrow Upon Humber

Pick Up All Litter

Pick up litter, recycle it.
Stop the war,
You're making a mess.
We need to pick up
The mess you have made.
Please do not throw
Litter on the ground.

Rebecca Millington (7)
John Harrison CE Primary School, Barrow Upon Humber

Flowers

Buy seeds for flowers to grow,
Because they all come in different colours
And they make your garden look pretty.
First you water them, then leave them in the sun.
They come in these colours:
Red, yellow, purple, blue and white.

Anya Portess (7)
John Harrison CE Primary School, Barrow Upon Humber

Animals

Animals can be saved,
Give them food to survive.
Farmers and zookeepers,
Look after your animals.
Keep animals safe!
It's really important!

Matthew Plastow (7)
John Harrison CE Primary School, Barrow Upon Humber

Homeless Animals

Falling trees like a lion's roar,
Bugs running from extinction,
A gunshot, then a howl,
A roar, then a fire,
Nowhere for them to live or breed,
What will happen when none are left?

Shaun Smith (10)
John Harrison CE Primary School, Barrow Upon Humber

Climate Change

All that pollution in the sky
Spreads its wings, for it can fly.
All this heat goes to the cold
Without the animals being told.
So what do you think to this terrible disgrace?
Do you want death to decide its face?

Cameron May (10)
John Harrison CE Primary School, Barrow Upon Humber

The Rainforest

In the rainforest,
The trees get chopped.
In the rainforest,
The rain makes the leaves
Come off the trees.
In the rainforest
Trees fall down and
It carries on raining.
Animals and bees will die
From rubbish and muck.
In the rainforest they
Are always flooded
All the time.
In the rainforest,
It's a disaster.

Kaleem Murphy (8)
Leeside Community Primary School, Heckmondwike

Rainforest

In the rainforest,
The trees get chopped.
In the rainforest
The crops grow tall.
In the rainforest
The rivers go pop.
In the rainforest
The bees buzz.
In the rainforest
The leaves flow.

Jamie Hanson (9)
Leeside Community Primary School, Heckmondwike

Rainforest

The environment needs you
To stop cutting down trees!
You're killing animals and bees!
The trees are getting chopped down.
If there are no trees, we will give a frown.
The rainforest deserves a crown.
The rainforest is the best in the town!
In the rainforest it gives out oxygen,
In the rainforest birds are flying,
So please, stop cutting down trees.

Elliott Campbell (8)
Leeside Community Primary School, Heckmondwike

The War

You get hurt by guns and killed by floods,
You get hurt by bombs and killed by knives.
You might get hurt by swords,
Also you get hurt because of the people
Who want to destroy their country.
And you can get killed by tanks,
You also can get killed by a boulder.
You can get shot by a gun,
You can get killed with a dagger.

Lauren Taylor (9)
Leeside Community Primary School, Heckmondwike

War

You can get killed by knives,
You can get killed because
People want to kill you.
You can get thrown out
And become homeless.
You can get hurt by army tanks.
You can get killed by guns,
You can get killed by any weapons,
You can get killed by bombs.

Curtis Smith (9)
Leeside Community Primary School, Heckmondwike

Animals And Extinction

Don't take elephant tusks, it's cruel,
If you do you're a fool.
Never throw metal drink cans,
It won't give turtles a hand.

If you shoot down a bear
It will mean you do not care.
Bees are going
And pollution is growing.

Molly Jones (9)
Leeside Community Primary School, Heckmondwike

Recycling

Put the paper in a paper bin,
Put the litter in a bag and recycle.
Recycling bin bags is a good idea.
If you don't, the bin will get more smelly.

Malaiqa Ahmed (8)
Leeside Community Primary School, Heckmondwike

Litter!

Don't litter, respect streets.
Litter can be any colour
But it will turn brown.
Don't litter, it will stab animals.
Don't litter if you want to be responsible.
The environment is well-known.
Don't litter, even if you think it's cool.
Litter is bad, so put it in the bin.

Paris Taylor (8)
Leeside Community Primary School, Heckmondwike

Extinct

Elephants' tusks are used,
Some animals are abused.
My fishes are dead,
The peacocks eat bread,
A snake gets stuck in a can,
Lizards never get a tan.
Knocking down trees,
Soon there will be no bees.

Rebecca Marples (8)
Leeside Community Primary School, Heckmondwike

Litter

Litter can be any colour
But it can turn brown.
Litter can be any shape,
Litter can be any size
But it can change to compost.
Litter can be a disaster.

Ellie Adams (8)
Leeside Community Primary School, Heckmondwike

The Rainforest

In the rainforest, the air is polluted.
In the rainforest trees are being chopped down.
In the rainforest the ground is going mouldy.
In the rainforest the animals are being killed by poachers.
In the rainforest the small animals are being crushed
By the trees that people are taking down.
In the rainforest there are only a few bees
Cos people are swatting them.

Bethan Jones (9)
Leeside Community Primary School, Heckmondwike

Bins

Paper to put in the paper bin,
Bins to put litter in,
Glass bin to put glass in,
Compost bin to make your own compost,
Fruit bin to put fruit in,
Bottle bin to put bottles in.
Put rubbish in the bin.

Ben Hardy (8)
Leeside Community Primary School, Heckmondwike

Rainforests

In the rainforest oxygen is going.
In the rainforest leaves are flowing.
In the rainforest animals are dying.
In the rainforest birds are flying.
In the rainforest trees are cut down.
In the rainforest we give a frown.

Joseph Smith (8)
Leeside Community Primary School, Heckmondwike

Litter

Litter, litter on the floor,
I see litter on the floor,
Cats chasing rats under mats,
Plastic on the doors.

Litter, litter on the floor,
I see litter on the floor.
I see pies on the floor,
Flies are on the door.

Litter, litter on the floor,
I see litter on the floor.
I see tins and bins,
And maggots on the door.

Litter, litter on the floor,
I see litter on the floor.
Cigarettes and glass on the floor,
Cat lying at the door.

Roisin Noonan (10)
Manor Leas Junior School, Lincoln

Save The World Today!

Somewhere in the world
Animals are dying from extinction.

Somewhere in the world
Someone is dying from rancid smoke
Billowing from chimneys
Making deadly storm clouds in the sky.

Somewhere in the world
Animals are being covered
In thick black tar.

So save the world . . . *today!*

Emily Elleray (10)
Manor Leas Junior School, Lincoln

Birds

There was a little pheasant
Flying in the sky,
Along came a shooter
And now it's in a pie.

There was a little robin
Living in a tree,
Along came a cat
And ate it for its tea.

There was a little duck
Swimming on the lake,
Along came a hunter
And now it's ready to bake.

There was a little blackbird
Sitting on a log,
Along came a wood-chopper
And now it's being eaten by a dog.

Crystal Wilson Clapham (9)
Manor Leas Junior School, Lincoln

Help The world

The world can be turned around
By us helping the environment!
Don't use the car,
Don't chop down trees,
Don't drop oil all over the place,
Be careful everywhere you go.
Think about it,
We can make a big difference.
Please help us!
Save the world, it's getting really bad.
Save the world!

Katharine Dawson-Meadows (9)
Manor Leas Junior School, Lincoln

Litter

Ants carry food up a tree,
But the naughty ants let the food free.
Loads of maggots, all on the floor,
There's a bin somewhere!

Litter, litter, it's everywhere,
Why is it so messy?
There's flies everywhere you go,
Cans, packets, cores and rats, anywhere you go.

Poor little animals trapped in litter,
Must be very scared.
Jars, packets and cores everywhere,
Litter is horribly bad.

Litter, litter, why must it be so horrible?
Poor animals getting hurt.
It's not fair, they didn't do anything wrong.
Litter is horribly bad.

Sasha Hate (9)
Manor Leas Junior School, Lincoln

Endangered

Somewhere in this world today
Animals have lost their homes.

Somewhere in the world today
Children are struggling to find clean water.

Somewhere in the world today
People don't have homes.

Somewhere in the world today
Trees are getting chopped down.

Stop it now!

Hollie Jepson (9)
Manor Leas Junior School, Lincoln

Endangered!

Somewhere in the world today
An animal struggles for survival.
He runs until he has to hide,
Until they finally find him.

Somewhere in the world today
A species breeds young,
They're out there somewhere though,
Hiding beneath the branches.

Somewhere in the world today
An animal dies young.
The mother tries to help,
Although they'll never be cured.

Somewhere in the world today
A monkey is in the zoo.
They're trying to breed them
So there will be more.

Greta Twine (9)
Manor Leas Junior School, Lincoln

How To Save The World

Stop killing our beautiful animals.
Start clearing up our litter and putting it in the bin.
Stop destroying our rainforest.
Start picking litter up off the ground, even if it's not yours.
Stop giving food to the ducks.
Start protecting our plants to keep our world living.
Stop wasting food, some people have nothing to eat.
Start to recycle rubbish and do not drop your rubbishy.
Stop wasting electricity because you have to pay for it.
Look after our planet to keep it healthy.

Aidan Stimson (8)
Manor Leas Junior School, Lincoln

Litter

Litter, litter everywhere,
Litter, litter on the floor,
But where?
Litter, litter by the door.

Litter, litter everywhere,
Litter, litter in the bins,
Litter, litter where?
Litter, litter with lots of tins.

Litter, litter everywhere,
By the bins are flying gnats.
Litter, litter where?
And by the bins are crawling rats

Litter, litter everywhere,
Litter, litter, it's a mess.
Litter, litter where?
Litter, litter, I wish there were less.

Lewis Smith (9)
Manor Leas Junior School, Lincoln

Save The Rainforests!

Don't cut down trees,
Don't murder animals,
Don't take away animals' homes.

Do enjoy the beauty,
Do let animals live in peace,
Do save the planet.

Let animals have oxygen,
Let birds have peace,
Let all animals live in peace.

James Waite (8)
Manor Leas Junior School, Lincoln

Litter

Litter, litter everywhere
On the floor.
I wonder where?
Near the door.

Litter, litter everywhere,
Animals better beware.
Apple core on the floor,
There'd better be no more.

Litter, litter everywhere,
There is jelly.
Animals better be aware,
It is turning smelly.

Litter, litter everywhere.
Eek! There is a dress,
I think the lady was thirty.
Oh what a mess.

Codie Paton (9)
Manor Leas Junior School, Lincoln

Somewhere In The World Today

Somewhere in the world today
A little child is sleeping on the street.

Somewhere in the world today
A monkey is dying from deforestation.

Somewhere in the world today
Fish are dying from cargo oil leaks.

Somewhere in the world today
People are discarding litter in rivers.

Thomas Bontoft (9)
Manor Leas Junior School, Lincoln

Pollution Everywhere

I'm a little animal
Running in the hedge,
Cut my feet on broken glass,
Soon I will be dead.

I'm a little animal
Running in a field,
Been poisoned by pesticides,
Soon I will be dead.

I'm a little animal
Swimming down the stream,
My fur is covered in oil,
Soon I will be dead.

I'm a little animal
Living in a tree,
My home got cut down,
Soon I will be dead.

Sophie Armitage (9)
Manor Leas Junior School, Lincoln

Earth Shouts 'Help!'

Somewhere in the world today
A lonely child is crying for clean water.

Somewhere in the world today
An old man is sitting on the street alone.

Somewhere in the world today
A child travelled through litter in a boat.

Somewhere in the world today
Everyone is shouting, 'Help!' and 'Thank you.'

Chloe Bedson (9)
Manor Leas Junior School, Lincoln

Somewhere In The World Today

Somewhere in the world today
A child walks alone
Along the litter
That's piled everywhere.

Somewhere in the world today,
In the morning at 10 o'clock,
The skies are as dark as night,
Full of thick black smoke.

Somewhere in the world today
Boats sail everywhere,
Leaving trails of dark oil,
Killing every animal that gets covered.

Somewhere in the world today
Animals are suffering.
They are growing smaller,
Losing their food. Help them!

Hannah Newman (9)
Manor Leas Junior School, Lincoln

How To Save The World

First, stop dropping litter because
You don't want to live in a pile of rubbish.
Next, stop cutting down trees,
So animals don't lose their homes.
Stop using cars because they cause
Pollution that blows out of the exhaust pipe.
Stop killing precious animals for no reason.
Don't catch endangered fish so much,
So they don't become extinct.

Abby Wright (7)
Manor Leas Junior School, Lincoln

Save The Earth!

Dying,
Dropping litter.
Help us live,
For we all care.

Smoke,
No smoke.
Big grey clouds,
Say *no* to smoke.

Stop,
Stop it,
Just stop littering,
You're killing endangered animals.

She,
She is,
She is the,
She is the world!

Olivia Clinton (9)
Manor Leas Junior School, Lincoln

Pollution

P ollution is bad, it should stop
O il is bad for people
L ittering is a thing that people should stop
L ots of rubbish on the floor
U se recycling bins to put rubbish in
T ell your mum and dad what's happening
I n houses you can stop littering
O xygen is needed to breathe
N obody should be doing these bad things.

Ebonie Evans (8)
Manor Leas Junior School, Lincoln

Pollution And Litter

P ollution is killing us
O verflowing water
L aziness
L ittering, destroying
U nhappy
T hick black smoke
I gloos melting, rubbishy
O verflowing
N ot recycling.

L aziness
I gloos melting
T hick black smoke
T hrowing rubbish
E xtinguish
R ecycle.

Shianne Vanderhyden (8)
Manor Leas Junior School, Lincoln

Somewhere In The World Today

Somewhere in the world today
A child is struggling to find
Clean food and water.

Somewhere in the world today
Rancid smoke from chimneys makes
Horrid storm clouds in the sky.

Somewhere in the world today
Animals are struggling to swim
Through the horrible dark tar.

Somewhere in the world today
Street people are alone, with nothing
To drink and eat, and nothing to do.

Lewis Dixon (9)
Manor Leas Junior School, Lincoln

Don't Be Mean, Think Green

Don't chuck, don't throw away,
It can be used in another way.
Metal, glass, plastic and wood,
Can be made into something new, which is good.
Instead of going in the car,
Why not walk? It's not that far.
Cycling can be very quick,
Stops car fumes that make you sick.
Always turn off your lights
So polar bears can sleep at night.
If only we could all just see
What a happy place this world could be.
Use your brain
And think again.

Megan Dexter (10)
Manor Leas Junior School, Lincoln

Water!

Water, water everywhere,
It is here, it is there.
In your tap and in the river,
If you jump in, you shall shiver.

Water, water everywhere,
It is here, it is there.
On the crops on the land,
At the beach it cleans the sand.

Water, water everywhere,
It is here, it is there.
Oil and chemicals don't belong,
Unless we look after it,
Clean water will be gone.

Rhian Smith (10)
Manor Leas Junior School, Lincoln

Endangered

Monkeys'
Habitat destroyed,
Destroyed for cash,
Save the homeless monkeys.

Tigers,
Love tigers,
Save tigers' skin,
Don't hurt the tigers.

Rhinos,
Save rhinos,
Don't hurt rhinos,
Care for the rhinos.

Ebony Wilson (9)
Manor Leas Junior School, Lincoln

Litter, Litter

Litter, litter everywhere,
Animals had better be aware.
Apple core on the floor
And there'd better be no more.

Litter, litter everywhere,
Animals had better be aware,
Tins and bottles not in bins,
Think of all the nasty things.

Litter, litter everywhere,
Animals had better be aware,
Lots and lots of mess,
Think how many people will be depressed.

Abigail Tomlinson (9)
Manor Leas Junior School, Lincoln

Panda, Panda

Panda, panda eating bamboo,
Now they may not see you.
Panda, panda in China,
An area should get finer, finer.

Panda, panda eating bamboo,
Now they may not see you.
Cuddly and cute like a teddy,
And pandas will always be steady.

Panda, panda eating bamboo,
Now they may not see you.
Pandas, pandas are the best,
But they aren't protected by a nest.

Clayton Evan (10)
Manor Leas Junior School, Lincoln

Poor Old Earth

Somewhere in the world today
A poor old fish is dying
From the oil coming out of a boat,
Like a giant ink stain.

Somewhere in the world today
Dumpers pick up rubbish.
The rubbish is as tall as a house,
With the dumpers looking smaller.

Somewhere in the world today
Animals are dying,
Trees are being chopped down,
Birds are hardly flying.

Jack Forman (9)
Manor Leas Junior School, Lincoln

Litter

Don't
Trash everywhere,
It could harm.
Animals could get killed.

Nasty,
Goes around,
People all coughing,
Black, horrible, horrendous smoke.

Endangered
Animals hurt,
Homes cut down,
Nasty, cute animals endangered.

Georgina Quarmby (9)
Manor Leas Junior School, Lincoln

Endangered!

Somewhere in the world today,
Animals all alone, no food.
Somewhere in the world today,
No home, no life.

Somewhere in the world today,
Animals with destroyed habitats.
Somewhere in the world today,
Litter all around.

Somewhere in the world today,
Sea creatures covered in oil.
Somewhere in the world today,
Forests being cut down.

Kate Creasey (9)
Manor Leas Junior School, Lincoln

How To Save The World

First, put rubbish in the bin because
If you put it on the floor
Animals could choke and die.
Next, don't cut down trees in the peaceful forest
Because it's basically killing yourselves.
We breathe from trees and so do animals.
Don't, I repeat, don't waste food,
Some people don't have any food.
Don't kill animals, it worries people
And eventually they will become endangered.
Nobody wants to live in a world
That's like a rubbish tip.

Alice Twine (7)
Manor Leas Junior School, Lincoln

How To Save The World

Stop killing poor animals, keep them living.
Start protecting friendly plants
So we can have oxygen.
Stop dumping horrible litter on the floor.
Start grabbing dirty rubbish
To keep our world clean.
Stop leaving bright lights on,
To save electricity.
Start switching off shiny lights
To save our world.
Stop driving in cars to keep our air fresh.
Start walking so the world can be a better place.

Mia Horne (7)
Manor Leas Junior School, Lincoln

How To Save The World

First, stop littering because
We want to keep the world clean and tidy.
Don't waste valuable things,
We want to use things over and over again.
Be kind to animals, they're part of our environment.
Never smoke, the bad smoke
Is going into the air.
Stop destroying things,
We want to save the world.

Henry Jollands (7)
Manor Leas Junior School, Lincoln

Pollution Has To Stop

P ollution is bad, *stop*
O ut of the car and get walking
L ittering has to stop
L ying around, get out and save the environment
U se recycling, it makes the world a better place
T rees help us survive, stop chopping them down
I ncredible or not, we can save the world
O nly we can save the world
N ow is the time to stop littering and start cleaning up.

Harrison Wood (8)
Manor Leas Junior School, Lincoln

Save The World

W e need to save the world
A lways put rubbish in the bin
L ittering stops now
K illing is not good.

Gemma Martin (8)
Manor Leas Junior School, Lincoln

Pollution

P lease recycle instead
O f just putting rubbish in the bin
L ove the world with all your
L ife and be careful
U ntil you die
T he world needs you
I nstead of a car, walk
O r go on a bike
N ow you can do it!

Jade Rodgerson (8)
Manor Leas Junior School, Lincoln

How To Save The World

Stop chucking litter into the environment.
Start saving the forests, if you don't you're killing them.
Stop driving cars in the world.
Start cycling, it's healthy for us all.
Stop making too many fumes.
Start making non-leaking ships.
Stop burying and burning litter.
Start using things again and again.
We can all help our world stay clean.

Matthew McRobbie (7)
Manor Leas Junior School, Lincoln

Dying Children

Somewhere in the world today,
there will be a child sleeping on hay.
Children are dying every day,
even dying on your birthday.

Jack Houlton (9)
Manor Leas Junior School, Lincoln

Let's Recycle

R educe, reuse, recycle
E ven affecting the planet
C ollect, recycle
Y ou can help save the world
C an you do it?
L osing wildlife
I ntroducing pollution that kills
N o to killing wildlife
G oing to help save the world.

Bethannie Cook (8)
Manor Leas Junior School, Lincoln

Recycling

R ecycling
E ating
C ycling
Y ou use your legs
C ars not for use
L itter in bins
I llness
N o cans in bins
G o use bins.

Toby Evans (8)
Manor Leas Junior School, Lincoln

Pollution

P eople are being killed because of us
O nly we can stop it
L et's stop pollution
L et's start walking
U se a horse instead of driving
T ell people to make an effort
I ll people need help
O il is being put into lakes, it is killing the fish
N othing can stop us from making the world a better place.

Jessica Worrell (9)
Manor Leas Junior School, Lincoln

Pollution

Crying,
Trash everywhere,
Trees cut down,
Smoke pollution in the air.

Oil,
Animals dying,
Polluting the water,
Oceans bare and black.

Nathen Billard (9)
Manor Leas Junior School, Lincoln

I Don't Have A Home

Help,
I'm endangered,
Save me please,
Don't chop down trees.

Help,
I'm hungry,
I need food,
Help me, help you.

Elie Clark (9)
Manor Leas Junior School, Lincoln

Racism

We can stop racism,
We can avoid wars,
We can love each other,
We are all one world.

Don't judge by skin colour,
Don't judge by race,
Don't judge by religion,
Don't be racist!

Aydan Christopher (9)
Manor Leas Junior School, Lincoln

Planet Green

G reen is what our planet should be
R emember to recycle
E ating animals is cruel
E nd pollution *now*
N ow it's time to save the world.

Eleni Papaioannou (8)
Manor Leas Junior School, Lincoln

Racism

We are one world,
We are all together as one group,
We do not judge by race or colour
And we all love each other.

Let us live in peace,
Without war or hatred.
Let's all share beliefs
And ignore our different skin colours.

James Hobson (8)
Manor Leas Junior School, Lincoln

War

War, war everywhere,
Wars here and wars there,
Dead maids
Killed in air raids.

Soldiers shoot their guns,
People eat their buns.
Bombs banging,
People hanging.

Devon Chapman (10)
Manor Leas Junior School, Lincoln

Save The World And City!

Animals are losing their
Habitats in the world.
Birds need to have peace,
Not trees coming down.
Save their rainforest.

Macauley Webb (8)
Manor Leas Junior School, Lincoln

Stop War And Racism

Together we can stop war,
Together we can stop racism,
Together we can stop both,
Together we can help people.

If you stop racism, it will stop war.
If we do it quickly together, if we at least try,
Stop racism and bring war to a stop.
Let's make the world a great place.

George Flower (8)
Manor Leas Junior School, Lincoln

The Bottle Holder

The bottle holder kills birds,
The bottle holder does not hide,
The bottle holder on the side,
The bottle holder does not die.

The bottle holder does not do good,
The bottle holder does not wear a hood.
Help! Help! Cries from animals all around.
No one helps, but can you?

Connor Price (9)
Manor Leas Junior School, Lincoln

Save Our World

Do not throw your rubbish on the ground,
Save our world and recycle.
Take your bike to school, not your car.
Oils are spreading through our lakes.
Stop litter and save our world.

Matthew Flaherty (8)
Manor Leas Junior School, Lincoln

Save Our World

Somewhere in the world today
There is someone poor dying of toxic smoke.

Somewhere in the world today
There are machines piling rubbish on the beach.

Somewhere in the world today
There are factories puffing out smoke, making deadly clouds.

Help to save the world today.

Zach Peplinski (9)
Manor Leas Junior School, Lincoln

Racism

Don't take it out on people
Who have different coloured skin.
Don't say stuff that can
Hurt people's feelings.
Don't laugh at those who
Speak a different language to us.
Don't say racist words.
Fight against racism.

Elisa Melina (8)
Manor Leas Junior School, Lincoln

Fire

F ire is bad for the environment
I t kills people
R ecycle instead of throwing it in the river
E ating some animals is bad.

Save the world, *please help!*

Finn Foster (8)
Manor Leas Junior School, Lincoln

Racism

Don't take it out on people
Who have different skin to yours.
Don't say stuff that can
Hurt people's feelings.
Don't laugh at those who speak
A different language to you.
Don't say any racist words.
Fight against racism.

Jack Robinson (9)
Manor Leas Junior School, Lincoln

Somewhere In The World Today

Somewhere in the world today
Pollution is being caused,
Stormy clouds in the sky.
Somewhere in the world today
Litter is being thrown,
Piles of rubbish covering the world.
Somewhere in the world today
A child is dying because of filthy water.

Abbie Ellis (9)
Manor Leas Junior School, Lincoln

How To Save The World

Stop killing endangered animals.
Start collecting plants and animals.
Stop dumping litter all over our special planet.
Start being helpful and put rubbish in the bin.
Stop wasting electricity.
Start tidying up the world.

Matthew Risebrow (7)
Manor Leas Junior School, Lincoln

Save The Rainforests

Don't cut down the trees,
No oxygen for animals.
Don't murder animals,
Don't take animals' homes!
Save our world.
Let animals have their homes,
Let people enjoy the rainforests,
Let birds have peace.

William French (8)
Manor Leas Junior School, Lincoln

Recycling

R ecycling is right
E verybody needs to start caring
C an you help me recycle as much as possible?
Y ou can make the world a better place
C an you help the poor animals that are going to be extinct?
L et's start now
E verybody can make a difference.

Charlie Turner (9)
Manor Leas Junior School, Lincoln

Pollution

We can all help stop pollution.
We can all save the day.
We can all save the human race.
We can all stop the horrible wars.
We can stop the world dying.
We can stop the horrendous dumping.
We can all be safe and happy every day.

Michael Nott (8)
Manor Leas Junior School, Lincoln

Big Bad Factory!

This factory is a disgrace,
We have to make it a better place.
The factory is a horrid sight
Late at night,
But some people think it's all right!
All the chemicals are coming out with a puff,
Kids hate this stuff!

Jasmine Greenhalgh (8)
Manor Leas Junior School, Lincoln

Save Our Planet

Together let's stop pollution!
Together we can save the world.
Together we can stop the devastating dumping of waste.
Together we can save the human race.
Together we can recycle rubbish.
Together we can help animals not to be murdered.
Together we can stop people doing racism and horrendous war.

Charlotte Parker (9)
Manor Leas Junior School, Lincoln

How To Save The World

Stop killing animals for their fur.
Stop smoking because it doesn't do any good.
Stop dumping rubbish in the ground.
Stop cutting down trees.
Stop using cars, just use cars for emergencies.
Stop wasting electricity.
Start to look after the world.

Joshua Scrimshaw (7)
Manor Leas Junior School, Lincoln

Come On, Recycle

Recycle, there's litter everywhere.
Recycle, there is loads.
Recycle, it's fun.
Recycle, not dump in rivers, lakes and seas.
Recycle tins, cans, glass, paper and wood.
Recycling saves the world.
Recycle, everyone can do it!

Lia Clark (8)
Manor Leas Junior School, Lincoln

Don't Make More Pollution

Don't be lazy,
Don't dump on the streets
Or in rivers!
Don't cut down trees!
Don't disturb animals sleeping.
Don't make pollution a bigger problem.
Recycle!

Liam Conlon-Bell (8)
Manor Leas Junior School, Lincoln

Recycle!

R ecycle please
E mpty bins,
C ars, leave at home, walk instead
Y ou should use bins
C ans, put in bins
L itter, don't throw on the floor
E ating, once done, use the bin not the floor.

Jake Goddard (8)
Manor Leas Junior School, Lincoln

How To Save The World

Stop throwing litter on the road.
Start putting your litter in the bin.
Stop wasting things or you won't be happy.
Start walking if you can, to be healthy.
Stop wasting electricity.
Start recycling your rubbish.
Stop cutting down trees.

Chloe Lambert (7)
Manor Leas Junior School, Lincoln

Help Us Save The World

H elp us save the world
E veryone can help us save the world
L et's help save the world
P ollution is very bad for the environment

U se your hands to pick up for the world
S ave the world.

Ryan Hird (8)
Manor Leas Junior School, Lincoln

Recycle

Recycle paper, cans and glass.
Recycle, so we don't pollute the world.
Recycle, so we don't kill the animals in the rivers.
Recycle, save the planet.
Recycle, don't hurt the environment.
Recycle because it is fun.

Sophie Connell (9)
Manor Leas Junior School, Lincoln

Litterbugs

L ook after our world
I magine the world clear of litter
T idy up the streets and your mess
T reat the world with respect
E nough of your rubbish
R educe your litter.

Kieron Price (7)
Manor Leas Junior School, Lincoln

Come On, Recycle

Recycle, there's litter everywhere.
Recycle, there is loads.
Recycle, it is fun.
Recycle, not throw in lakes, seas and rivers.
Recycle cans, tins, glass, paper and wood.
Recycle, everyone can do it.

Khye Espin-Shaw (8)
Manor Leas Junior School, Lincoln

How to Save The World

Stop killing endangered animals.
Start saving animals' homes.
Stop chopping trees down,
Start saving trees.
Stop dumping rubbish.
Start recycling.

Daniel Smith (7)
Manor Leas Junior School, Lincoln

Litter Is Bad

L itter kills animals
I ll people need help
T ry to walk
T ry to stop pollution
E verybody needs to stop pollution
R ecycle recycling materials.

Benjamin Skinner (8)
Manor Leas Junior School, Lincoln

Carbon Dioxide

C lear up all the mess we've got to breathe
A nd leave the trees alone, don't cut the leaves
R otten people cut down trees
B e nice to plants, they give us air
O h, but some people just don't care
N o, no, no, don't cut them down

D anger for us if you cut down trees
I for one say no to people who cut down trees
O h no, don't hurt them
X xx, it's mostly men
I f you stop all this then our world will be great
D on't care what some people think
E ek, stop it, don't do that!

Elizabeth Limbert (9)
Pollington-Balne CE Primary School, Nr Goole

Global Warming

G etting hotter every day
L ife will be destroyed some day
O zone layer melting away
B ut can be saved if we have less airways
A ll to blame
L et's have an aim

W arm Earth getting hotter
A nd also lots of flood water
R ound the world not just here
M ore and more it affects here
I n this world there's people that suffer
N ot just us but animals like cheetahs and beavers
G o on, help the world.

Alex Austrums (10)
Pollington-Balne CE Primary School, Nr Goole

The RRR

The first R is for reduce
The second R is for reuse
And the third R is for recycle
Reduce, reuse, recycle
Reduce petrol and use sunflower oil
Reuse buttons and bottles
Recycle cardboard and paper
If you don't reduce, reuse or recycle
You will damage the world
We need to know these words
Reduce, reuse, recycle
Come on and recycle every day
Reduce, reuse, recycle.

William Haggar (8)
Pollington-Balne CE Primary School, Nr Goole

Pollution

Pollution, pollution
Why is it here?
Pollution, pollution
It is everywhere
Pollution, pollution
Day and night
Pollution, pollution
Stop, right there!

Mae-Louise Hitchen (9)
Pollington-Balne CE Primary School, Nr Goole

Recycle

R ubbish
E nvironment
C ans
Y ou can help
C ardboard
L eaves
E ncourage.

Courtney Shaw (8)
Pollington-Balne CE Primary School, Nr Goole

Environment

Do not shoot eagles because it is illegal
Do not steal their eggs, they could break their legs
The environment is very cool
It is bigger than a school
The world is getting hotter
So help the nice otters
They live in water, not a lot of dishwater.

Kieran Blackburn (8)
Pollington-Balne CE Primary School, Nr Goole

The Soldiers

War could stop
And the soldiers come home
No more bombs
No more killings
People living in
Peace.

Peter Buckley (9)
Pollington-Balne CE Primary School, Nr Goole

The Recycle Bin

R is for reduce, save things that you use
R is for reuse things again
R is for recycle, put things in the bin
Reduce, reuse, recycle
I am the rubbish bin sitting on the street
I like it though because I get lots of food.

Tadhg Keelan Parker-Walker (8)
Pollington-Balne CE Primary School, Nr Goole

Why?

War, war, they knock at my door
Machine guns blasting
Bombs dropping
Planes falling, people dying
Children crying
Why?

Harry Free (8)
Pollington-Balne CE Primary School, Nr Goole

Pick Up Your Litter

Don't throw your litter on the floor
Put it in the bin when you open the front door
The world is a nightmare
When us humans come along
If you put your litter in the bin
Our world will be a much happier place to live in.

Maisie Louisa Nicholson (8)
Pollington-Balne CE Primary School, Nr Goole

War

People fighting, children crying, people dying
Soldiers afraid, soldiers scared, soldiers dying
People shooting, people injured, people sad
Soldiers bombing, people bleeding, people terrified
People scared, people scared, people helping to kill.

Poppy Farrell (7)
Pollington-Balne CE Primary School, Nr Goole

Stop

Children crying and people dying
Soldiers fighting, soldiers crying
Soldiers bombing, soldiers shooting, why?
We need to stop war!

Ben Kiddy (8)
Pollington-Balne CE Primary School, Nr Goole

Recycling

Metal skips all in a line
Bottles, cans
Plastic please
Waiting for a hungry feed
Fill me, fill me
Hurry, please.

Coloured boxes in a line
Brown for paper
Green for tins
Plastic, glass can all go in
Waiting for a hungry feed
Do your bit
Recycle please!

Abbie Crossley (10)
Ryhill J&I & Nursery, Ryhill

My Poem

The world would be a better place if . . .
People allowed animals to roam in their space.

The world would be a better place if . . .
Factories didn't pollute the open space.

The world would be a better place if . . .
Rubbish wasn't chucked all over the place.

The world would be a better place if . . .
People didn't fight and spoke face to face.

Callum Burton (10)
Ryhill J&I & Nursery, Ryhill

Polluting Our Planet

Ice melting
Ozone breaking
People making litter
Trees are falling
Animals dying
And lots of dirty water
Toxic dumping
Smoke coming
Earth becoming warmer
It's time to act
That's the fact!

Christine Agagon (10)
St Paulinus RC Primary School, Dewsbury

End All War

I'm in the war,
I hate to fight.
I rest all day,
And work all night.
I kill people who could be family,
I don't like this, have I got insanity?
It's not fair to fight and kill,
Because we end up in coffins and holes that fill.
Can we just end this unmerciful war?

Bethany Whitelock (11)
St Paulinus RC Primary School, Dewsbury

Global Warming

Electric off
You will save
Water off
You will save
Gas off
You will save
You will save people
You will save animals
You will save everything!

Elizabeth Jennings (10)
St Paulinus RC Primary School, Dewsbury

Unsafe War

Cruelty
Burnt houses
Dead people
Endangered animals
Hurt families
Sick children
Unsafe
War!

Lauren Foxton (10)
St Paulinus RC Primary School, Dewsbury

Animal Hunting · Haiku

People have to stop
Do not kill an animal
It is cruel to them.

Courtney Hewitt (10)
St Paulinus RC Primary School, Dewsbury

Crashing And Killing!

Lights flashing
Sirens ringing
Cars speeding
Glass shattering
People weeping
Yes, another person
Killed!

Fay Kilburn (10)
St Paulinus RC Primary School, Dewsbury

Global Warming

Lights beaming
Litter falling
Cooling towers steaming
Water splashing
Trees crashing
We must stop
Now!

Madeleine Parkin (10)
St Paulinus RC Primary School, Dewsbury

The Dying Earth

Leaving lights on
Throwing away, not recycling
Not using both sides of paper
Leaving taps on when not used
Cutting down trees
Watching too much TV
Not recycling!

Hannah Riordan (10)
St Paulinus RC Primary School, Dewsbury

Stop Pollution!

The world is ruined
Because it is polluted
Help stop it today!

If we recycle
With all our bits and bobs
We could save the world!

Natalie Taylor (10)
St Paulinus RC Primary School, Dewsbury

The Rainforest

The strong smell of thick wet bark
The birds and animals singing
The blue, dazzling, crystal river
Rushing waterfalls
Hidden remedies and discoveries to be found
You kill the rainforest and you kill the Earth.

Chloe Render (10)
St Paulinus RC Primary School, Dewsbury

Pollution Can Stop Now!

Animals are in danger
Because of pollution
We are harming ourselves
By harming the environment
We are polluting the seed of life
It can stop now!

Corey Blades (10)
St Paulinus RC Primary School, Dewsbury

Recycling · Haiku

Try and recycle
Stop, you will wreck the planet
Don't destroy the world.

Paris Bowler (10)
St Paulinus RC Primary School, Dewsbury

The War · Haiku

The war is nasty
The war is bad, don't do it
Help stop it today.

Joe Longstaff (10)
St Paulinus RC Primary School, Dewsbury

Planet Earth · Haiku

It's almost too late
But if we start helping now
We could save the Earth.

Liam Conway (10)
St Paulinus RC Primary School, Dewsbury

War · Haiku

My boy is out there
But no one really cares
Please think about them.

Bradley Hatfield (10)
St Paulinus RC Primary School, Dewsbury

Look After Our World

Look after our world
Today and tomorrow
Our world is sad
Full of sorrow
We can do it
If we work together
So it stays happy
Forever and ever.

Recycling is good
Wasting is bad
All this rubbish
Is making me mad
Trees and plants
They're being cut down
Car fumes and more
Are hanging around.

So remember . . .
Look after our world
So it's not sad
Or full of sorrow
We can do it, if we work together
To keep our world safe forever and ever.

Ella Verity (10)
St Wilfrid's Catholic Primary School, Sheffield

Rainforest Destruction Poem

Day by day our rainforests are shrinking
Men are just ruining the Earth, are they thinking?
The oxygen is going, animals are dying
When will the woodcutters stop denying?
The rainforest is empty, how can this be?
Will anyone ever listen to me?

Oliver Fernandes (10)
St Wilfrid's Catholic Primary School, Sheffield

Sea Pollution

What does it feel like?
A black hole in the middle without no riddle
It's mad, it's sad
The fish are dying while animals are crying
What can we do?
Polluting the sea, all because of me
It's mad, it's sad
It's black and dusty and really crusty
Why is it happening?
I've cared, now I'm really scared
It's sad, it's mad
It's not fun, look what you've done!
Why is death here?
Death is near, death is nearly here
It's so sad, it's mad
All the sadness in me
I will turn into a green-black sea
Stop polluting the sea, you're killing me.

Hannah Cowling (9)
St Wilfrid's Catholic Primary School, Sheffield

Mega Meltdown

Mega meltdown coming, what do we do?
Save our planet that's what we do.
Stop polluting, stop the cars tooting
And help the polar bears, they're on thin ice
They're heavier than mice
So don't just stand there
Help them if you dare
Mega meltdown coming
You know what to do
And here's our last words for you
Reduce, reuse and recycle.

William Quinn (7)
St Wilfrid's Catholic Primary School, Sheffield

Save The Rainforest

S ave the rainforest
A nimals try to limp to safety
V ans come to cut down trees
E very animal deserves a life

T he chainsaws are devouring their trees
H abitats are being destroyed
E verything in the rainforest needs to change

R ainforests should be better than this
A nimals will soon be extinct
I f we don't work together
N othing will change
F or the animals
O rang-utans are soon to die out
R ecycle paper so the trees can stay
E veryone needs to help
S o the rainforest is a better place
T he rainforest needs to stay!

Tom Pathe & Alex Moone (10)
St Wilfrid's Catholic Primary School, Sheffield

Don't Be An Environmental Bully

Don't cut the rainforest down
Or the world will end up with a frown
Even though it's dangerous in there
You should put in a lot of care
So don't be an environmental bully
We don't want to be without air
Or our lives will be left to tear
If everything will be destroyed
Every bit and every stone
Everything and everyone
Will always be alone.

Matthew Dewhurst (9)
St Wilfrid's Catholic Primary School, Sheffield

Don't Be Bleak · Use Your Feet!

Our world is a disgrace, it's murky and it's brown
We're all very unhappy, it just makes us frown
We're using too much energy, as well as all the oil
If we use our cars too much this year
Our world will start to spoil.

What happens when there's no more fuel?
We won't be able to drive to school
So let's start now and make our world great
Start to walk, before it's too late.

No war, no more pollution
We have the perfect solution
Our world will have cleaner air
Be multicoloured and we still start to care
Us eco-kids want you to know
We are ready, so let's go!

Catherine Pickin, Anna Wrench & Kate McKerrow (10)
St Wilfrid's Catholic Primary School, Sheffield

Raging Rainforest

The rainforest should be blooming
With exotic birds to pumas
But we're being blind and very unkind
We're chopping down trees
For our unimportant needs
We're using up Earth's fuels
Digging with greediness for jewels
We're corrupted and animals are in pain
Stop, think, in a few years to come
Hear the trickle of water and animal babies having fun
If we work together we will see this through
And you will see what little actions can do!

**Patrick O'Sullivan, Jack Shield,
Euan McClafferty & Joe Curtis (10)**
St Wilfrid's Catholic Primary School, Sheffield

Save Our World!

Our world is a great big place
But we're doing something wrong
It's turning into a disgrace
With litter everywhere
And pollution in the air
So let's get recycling, to make it fair
Our rainforest too is feeling sad
People are cutting down trees
And are not feeling bad
All our furniture is made out of logs
No one's feeling sorry for the little tiny frogs
Our world is a great big place
If we do something right
It will put a big happy smile
On its face.

Nuala Pepper (9)
St Wilfrid's Catholic Primary School, Sheffield

Recycle, Do Your Bit To Save The World!

Recycle, do your bit to save the world
If we work together as a team
We can make our world gleam
Landfill sites are overflowing
In the bin your rubbish is going
If we get our act together
Our world will be clean forever
There are black bins, blue bins, green bins and more
If we recycle, the world will be better I'm sure
Reduce, reuse, recycle
Let's carry on with this cycle
If we believe in ourselves to make this world a happier place
We will get a big smile on our face
recycle, do your bit to save the world!

Amy Hughes (10)
St Wilfrid's Catholic Primary School, Sheffield

Recycle!

Reduce plants
Reuse bags
And recycle paper
You should cycle
You should recycle
Put it in the recycling bin
And don't forget not to use cars
Remember
Don't worry you can recycle it
You can recycle lots of things
Like glass, plastic, cardboard
And lots more things
We need you to help us recycle
Remember, so save the big wide world
So recycle.

Louisa Edwardson (7)
St Wilfrid's Catholic Primary School, Sheffield

Recycle!

Recycle, recycle, do it now
There's no time to mess around
If there's anything you don't want or don't need
Give them to a recycle bin, they do need a feed
The amount of dropping litter has increased to 99
If you recycle the Earth will be fine
All animals are choking, dying every day
When you recycle it will go a very long way
Recycle, recycle, it's our time
I'm sick of this, Earth's full of grime
Glass, plastic and cardboard too
Recycle everything, it's down to you
We love our world and everyone in it
All this litter, none of it fits!

Madeleine Eddleston (10)
St Wilfrid's Catholic Primary School, Sheffield

You'll Regret

Our planet Earth please protect
If you don't you'll regret
When all life's dead and gone
And the world looks like it's been hit
By a giant bomb.

You'll regret
The way you chop down every tree
And use up all the energy
The way you hurt the wildlife
And start all the pain and strife.

And you'll regret
You'll regret
Oh, you will regret.

Louis Westoby (11) & Edmund Tooley (10)
St Wilfrid's Catholic Primary School, Sheffield

Save The Ice!

The ice is breaking
Seas are rising
Polar bears are in danger
There are less and less
Stop this mess

So we need your help if this is to be dealt
And think, think, think
And the ice won't shrink, shrink, shrink.

So turn off lights, don't get into fights
Use less fuel, cycle to school

Turn off the TV and . . . think
Save the ice!

Katherine Atkin (9)
St Wilfrid's Catholic Primary School, Sheffield

Save The Sea

Stop sea pollution, save the fish
We can do it, we don't need a wish
Sharks will perish, whales will die
To stop this we have to work hard and try.

Factories dump chemicals and rubbish in the sea
We have to stop it, you and me
Lots of litter is dumped in the oceans
It has got to stop.

The water will turn black and brown
When we can swim or fish, we will frown
It will be our fault, can't you see?
Stop killing fish, save the sea.

Tom Hardwick (9)
St Wilfrid's Catholic Primary School, Sheffield

Save The Rainforests

Don't destroy the rainforest
It is a tropical place
It takes a long time for one to grow
It could affect the human race.

Don't destroy the world
Animals are going bare
So start recycling
Or there will be no clean air.

Don't destroy the universe
Look at the bad state
So save the world now
Before it gets too late.

Edward Blythe (10)
St Wilfrid's Catholic Primary School, Sheffield

Shrinking The Polar World

People are shrinking the polar world
The polar region is shrinking if we don't act quickly
The meltdown is coming
So save the polar region
So hurry up and try and save the polar region.

Ice is getting thinner
Because we're not helping
We're going to save the polar world
So let's get going.

We have to start using less steam
We have to cut electricity
Then we can save the polar world.

Liam Jackson (8)
St Wilfrid's Catholic Primary School, Sheffield

Save And Recycle

S ave the trees
A land will get sea
V illains are the saws
E veryone will get full jaws

&

R ecycle more bottles
E veryone wastes bottles
C an you save the environment?
Y elp, will say the animals
C ould the world be saved?
L ittle time is left
E ndangered animals are dying, let's save the world!

Matt Cooper (9)
St Wilfrid's Catholic Primary School, Sheffield

Let's Get Thinking!

The babies are crawling and the toddlers are squirming
But the meltdown is coming so let's get running.

Let's all play our part using all of our hearts
The polar region is shrinking, so let's get thinking

Hurry up and grab your coat
While I will go and get some much needed help

And let's bike to school and save some fuel
Look out, the meltdown is about
The ice is shrinking because we are not really thinking

Save the world and save yourself
And save those poor animals that are becoming extinct.

Eloise Brennan (9)
St Wilfrid's Catholic Primary School, Sheffield

Stop, Don't Drop

Recycle your rubbish for it to be used again
Because it will be melted down
Turned into papers, bottles and tins
Reuse the things that you want to take away
For other people, reduce, reuse, recycle.

Reduce waste, reuse - don't just throw away
Charity shops - recycle - use the Internet to recycle
Reduce, reuse, recycle
Don't put your bottles in the bin
Smash them in the recycling bin
If you don't, it's a sin
Reduce, reuse, recycle.

Luke Baldrey (8)
St Wilfrid's Catholic Primary School, Sheffield

Mr Bean

Mr Bean was extremely green
Out of all the animals in the rainforest he was never mean
He had two favourite slogans he said every day
They were, 'Save the day or you will pay,'
And, 'Stop chopping and recycle your shopping.'

Mr Bean could do everything, he really was the best
He used to smell sweet refreshing flowers
But now his heart aches with pain
Now he smells the vile rancid stench of poor hurt animals,
'Save the day or you will pay.'
'Stop chopping and recycle your shopping.'

Gerry McDonagh (11) Carl Gillespie,
Keiran Muter & Hakeem Ahmed (10)
St Wilfrid's Catholic Primary School, Sheffield

The World Can Change

Animals are dying
The world is crying
Animals are sad and moaning
The world is groaning.

We hear the trees come crashing down
This makes the world frown
We are devastated
Animal hunters are hated
But we can make the world better
We will try and send out a letter
All animals are thrilled and really glad they're not killed
So if we all work together the world will be happy forever.

Tullia Hinchliffe (10)
St Wilfrid's Catholic Primary School, Sheffield

Poachers, I Hate Them

Poachers are killing
They make me sad and angry
I need to scream at them,
Stop being cruel!'
They kill African animals
And look at what they've done!

Now they've stopped hunting
I am very happy with myself
The whole world helped me
They were sad
They said no to hunting
Finally they've stopped.

William Kidder (10)
St Wilfrid's Catholic Primary School, Sheffield

Save Our Planet!

Us eco children want to save our planet
Help us break this horrible habit
All the animals are weeping in pain
It's driving us lot very insane
And the planets are getting very unhappy
So come on, let's get snappy

Stop the pollution, pick up the litter
Hurry up and don't be bitter
We need to work together
To make the world happier for heaven's sake
Us eco children want to save our planet
Help us break this horrible habit!

Isabel Griffiths (11) & Francesca Gerrard (10)
St Wilfrid's Catholic Primary School, Sheffield

Planet Takeover

Don't cut our rainforests down
Do not use the precious wood
To make a fire
You'll help to heat the world
It will get pretty dire.

Do not use a lot of wood
Or we could die out
And the only thing on Earth will be
The sea creatures, don't cut trees down
Or we will lose our fruit
Please don't cut a lot of trees
Help save the world.

Laurence Plunkett (8)
St Wilfrid's Catholic Primary School, Sheffield

If You Don't Stop

Why kill all the animals for people to see?
Stop the chopping down, stop the chopping down
So why cut down all the trees just for you and me?
Stop the chopping down, stop the chopping down
Do you want all the monkeys and leopards to die?
Stop the chopping down, stop the chopping down
If you chop down all of the trees, you will have to say
Goodbye to all of the delicious fruit such as bananas, coconuts
Melons, water melons, mangoes and much more
Stop the chopping down, stop the chopping down
Would you cut down the rainforest and lose all of this?
So stop the chopping down now!

Phoebe Robertson (9)
St Wilfrid's Catholic Primary School, Sheffield

Our Rainforest

As the chainsaws devour the trees
The animals and insects are trying to flee
Before we destroy and kill another
Let's try and give them cover
When their habitats and homes are dying
At least they know that we are trying
We will hear them cry in pain
That will drive others madly insane
We could try to *recycle* not litter
That would make the world not be bitter
So all you choppers go away
Leave the trees or you will pay!

Alfie Chester & Rory O'Sullivan (10)
St Wilfrid's Catholic Primary School, Sheffield

We Need To Change This!

The skies are polluted, the birds are dying
We need to change this so the birds are flying
The sea is dirty, green and black
We need the blue and clean sea back
The leaves on the trees are yellow and brown
Making the rainforest feel down
It's disappointing this wonderful world is being destroyed
But we need to change this, so it can be enjoyed
We need to smell the beautiful, healthy, fresh air
And hear the sounds of the animals everywhere
If we work together we can sort this issue out
Make the world safe to be about.

Lucy Turner (10)
St Wilfrid's Catholic Primary School, Sheffield

You Can Save The World

If you cut the rainforest down
You will make everyone frown
The birds, bees, plants and trees
If you don't do something we won't breathe.

If you torture the rainforest
you will pay the price
You will see it's not nice
You will regret it.

We chop down trees to make furniture
But buy some seeds, plant them please
It's for the sake of the human race.

Peter Murch (8)
St Wilfrid's Catholic Primary School, Sheffield

Save The Rainforest

Rainforests give oxygen, save the trees
If you cut down trees, save the trees
If you cut down trees that's not environmental
For all the trees are gentle

Trees give air, for all that's there
If trees die, you will die
Don't cut down all that's brown
Recycle very well, for all that has fell

Save the trees for all the air
That all the trees could be bare
Save the rainforest.

Isabella Breslin (8)
St Wilfrid's Catholic Primary School, Sheffield

Walking With The World

Hearing howls for help is driving me mad
We've let down the world and made it real sad
This could be the end of nature
We'll find a way but the problem's so major
We're so determined that . . .
We can work with the world to not use a car
Use your skills for cycling, it will take you just as far
The sound of birds singing is so sweet and clear
The catchy doorbell ringing is music to my ear
Go on the bus, if you're in a rush
We can save our world so come on, let's do it!

Hyunsu Doh (11) & Helen Alexander-Barnes (10)
St Wilfrid's Catholic Primary School, Sheffield

Use The Bins

Don't drop litter, it looks untidy, it creates a big mess
Help the features of the world
Recycle and tidy up
Don't leave glass, a kid could crash
Don't you know it leaves a rash
Put garden waste in a garden bin
Otherwise a rat could come
There's bins around, don't drop litter all around
The fumes could kill off plants and bugs
Rats could leave germs because of your litter
Help look after the world.

Alice Sullivan (7)
St Wilfrid's Catholic Primary School, Sheffield

Don't Drop Litter

Don't drop litter on the ground
Because there's a bin around
Rats and rats will gather together
And start ripping the litter
Glass and glass with smash and smash
And danger will come closer and closer
Ignore it at your peril
So watch out for the threat
Because it could kill habitats
So please don't drop litter
Or you will make us bitter.

Finlay James (8)
St Wilfrid's Catholic Primary School, Sheffield

River Pollution

Rivers are being polluted, can we stop it?
It's getting very bad, it's no longer just a bit
Fish are dying and being murdered by toxic waste
We should clean out those rivers, get at the poisonous taste
Twice a year is enough the rivers are really bad
It is extremely bad, everyone should be sad
Don't put litter in a river, how would you like it
If giants dropped things on your head?
Fishing is evil, why should we do it, why, why, why?
Think of the poor trout
People should be sorry and get all the waste out.

Daniel Mathews (9)
St Wilfrid's Catholic Primary School, Sheffield

The Big Green Recycle Poem

If you recycle, we will cycle
So we can save the environment
By everybody treasuring litter not trashing it
And everybody stopping frowning so much
In the bin, so you can be an eco-kid
But if you don't recycle
The world could be full of litter
So please treasure it
Don't, don't trash it
And don't put so much in the bin
Recycle, recycle.

Lucy Gretton (8)
St Wilfrid's Catholic Primary School, Sheffield

River Pollution

River pollution, animals are dying
River pollution, animals are crying
Destruction of habitats is terrible
It's smelly, deadly and horrible.

Scoop out litter and waste
At least it's easier than scooping out toothpaste
Stop pollution we'll give a fine
We all think it's unkind
Stop river pollution . . .
Now!

Claudia Llaca-Valeria (9)
St Wilfrid's Catholic Primary School, Sheffield

Green Rainforest

Trees are being chopped down
Butterflies will have to find another home
Birds and creatures won't have nests
all the other animals need to have some rests
Oh please don't chop the rainforest down
Oh please don't chop the rainforest down
For people that do, are a clown
That is wasting, you just recycle paper
Instead of chopping the trees down
We can save our planet!

Emily O'Brien (8)
St Wilfrid's Catholic Primary School, Sheffield

Take Action Now!

The dump is a horrible place, all it does is waste our space
It poisons animals as well, it gives off a terrible smell
It makes me upset to see, how sad our world can be
Our future is full of doom, our world is all grim and gloom
But here we come the eco-kids, the world's future depends on us
Recycle, reuse, reduce, all our happiness will be let loose
The grass will be fresh and green, the air will be sweet and clean
To do this all you need to do is think about what you use
And of course the most important thing
Take action now!

Alice O'Brien (10)
St Wilfrid's Catholic Primary School, Sheffield

Animals Are Losing Their Homes

Animals are losing their homes
We don't like it
Burrows are being raided
We don't like it
Animals are becoming extinct
We don't like it
Owls are losing their nests in trees
We don't like it
People think they need more space
We don't like it!

Vivien Uttley (8)
St Wilfrid's Catholic Primary School, Sheffield

Rainforest Scene Is Green

The rainforest is home to lots of species
But if you chop it down they won't see me
From big, big leaves with tiny spiders
To tiny logs with great big tigers
The rainforest gives oxygen for everyone to breathe
So if they disappear they might lose all their leaves
If you stop and think a while
The rainforest will be gone
The big green poetry machine improves it a lot
Why don't you join in and have a lot of fun?

Emily Catherine Parker (8)
St Wilfrid's Catholic Primary School, Sheffield

A Polluted Pond

There is a polluted pond with fish and frogs
But they are all dying, I am so not lying
Newts and water snails all around
There are quite a lot I have found
Filters and bubbles greasy with slime
Almost the colour of a lime
Bugs in the water all creepy and crawly
I just realised they are all very poorly
There is a polluted pond, I am very sad
I wish I didn't get even more mad.

Trishali Fernando (9)
St Wilfrid's Catholic Primary School, Sheffield

River Pollution

Stop this pollution now
Create new habitats
Clean the rivers
Rescue the animals
We need your help to stop these machines
So let's get rid of the toxic, the red, the brown
And put in the blue, the green, the fish, the frogs
Please help, it makes you feel sad
It's very bad
Please help now!

Joey Humphreys (9)
St Wilfrid's Catholic Primary School, Sheffield

River Pollution

River pollution is so disgraceful
River pollution is most irritable
How can we stop this madness?
This gives Earth creatures great sadness
We cannot deny it
And do not try it
Stop river pollution now
We must act now
Please stop it
Please stop it now!

Morgan Barrott
St Wilfrid's Catholic Primary School, Sheffield

Reduce, Reuse, Recycle

Reduce, recycle your rubbish
Reuse old things
recycle your bottles
Don't throw them in the bin
You can have hours of fun
Smashing, not to is a sin
Recycling things is good
Then you won't have to put it in the mud
You will have so much fun
So reduce, reuse and recycle.

Joe Pepper (8)
St Wilfrid's Catholic Primary School, Sheffield

Use Your Feet

We're the bosses, so do what we say
We are going to make some changes today
Don't use wheels because they're not cool
Use your feet because they rule
The car may be fast
But would you rather want the planet to last?
So if we do it all together
We can make the planet last forever
So stop the world from turning black
And come on, let's bring the colours back.

Lydia McGuinness & Niamh Murphy (10)
St Wilfrid's Catholic Primary School, Sheffield

Litter

If the world was full of litter
I would not be pleased
The bins are there for a reason
You should put the litter in a bin
You will not be happy
If the rivers are flowing with rubbish
The fish will die
You won't be able to swim
With all that junk
There won't be any fish to buy.

Scarlett Jessop (7)
St Wilfrid's Catholic Primary School, Sheffield

Rainforest Destruction

Rainforest destruction, what a terrible thing
The poor trees are getting chopped down
Animals' habits are dying out
Nowhere to live, no food to eat . . .
The lungs of the world have difficulty breathing
It should stop now!
Stop destroying the trees, they are all dying out
And we can make the river blue and clean
Let's make the sun shine on trees
Let's save the rainforest now!

Chiara Natasha Hinchcliffe (10)
St Wilfrid's Catholic Primary School, Sheffield

Save The Rainforest

I came here to tell you the rainforest is in a state
So don't cut down the trees
Or get rid of the birds and bees
So try and recycle
To save the rainforest water cycle
Rebel against the log cutters
Or it may lead to be the end of our planet
Don't destroy habitats
Or part of the world's beautiful colours and flowers
So *save the rainforest!*

Aaron Robert Jessop (9)
St Wilfrid's Catholic Primary School, Sheffield

Rainforest

Rainforests have lots of trees but people keep on cutting them down
Stop the chop or we all will suffer
Without our rainforests we all will run out of oxygen
So please, please, please, just help us survive
And we could have some better lives
But some of us aren't doing it
Our lives would be better if we keep plants
Don't be silly, just give it a try
And the world will change
So start to try to stop chopping trees down.

Sam Gamblin (7)
St Wilfrid's Catholic Primary School, Sheffield

Recycling

If the world was made of litter
I would not be pleased
Because there would be no trees
Get rid of it, recycle it
Do all you can to stop
Because you will save a flower shop
Just imagine littered seas
It could cause a very bad disease
Do not drop litter or you would not be pleased
When all you find is a land of no bushes and trees.

Vinnie Kenny (7)
St Wilfrid's Catholic Primary School, Sheffield

Save Our Rainforest

R ecycle and you could help
A nimals are dying
I ffy, horrible and disgusting
N o littering in our world
F orests are getting cut down
O ut of everyone in the world you could do your bit
R euse, reproduce
E nvironment will die if you don't help
S ave our world
T ogether!

Cameron Bradley (11)
St Wilfrid's Catholic Primary School, Sheffield

Save Our World

Do not waste an onion skin
If you want to save the world
Put it in your compost bin
If you've been using a tomato soup tin
Recycle it, do not sin.

Look at all the rubbish, like landfill sites
Creating pollution, day and night
The world is turning brown and green
But we can make our world clean!

Eoin Doyle (9)
St Wilfrid's Catholic Primary School, Sheffield

Make The Rainforest Green!

Trees are being chopped down
Bees don't have a home
Animals want them back
Oh please don't let them go.

We try to teach education
But all we make is a horrible occasion
The trees want a friend
Oh please don't make them bend.
Save our planet!

Rachel Dewhurst (8)
St Wilfrid's Catholic Primary School, Sheffield

Save The Rainforest

You can save the rainforest that is very green
It is like a big machine
It has lots of trees
That give us lots of bees
Lots of different flowers
That have healing powers
Recycle stuff that would be good
That's why you should
Save the rainforest!

Amy Barnett (8)
St Wilfrid's Catholic Primary School, Sheffield

Save The Rainforest!

There are so many lovely things
All the things that are alive
Don't cut down or trees will frown
Oxygen wasted for paper
Or go in the chamber down below
The animal world will be gone
If you don't stop
Don't you dare hurt the animal kingdom
See what I mean and *stop!*

Tom Brennan-Procter (9)
St Wilfrid's Catholic Primary School, Sheffield

Rubbish!

We don't want anybody to throw glass
Litter is dangerous for people
If you pick it up
You could cut yourself and bleed
If animals eat a lot of plastic
They could choke and die
Litter is a waste of things
So let's keep our planet clean
Let's try!

Archie Braddock (7)
St Wilfrid's Catholic Primary School, Sheffield

Animals Need Help

Animals need our help
Don't kill, help them and yelp
Help other people to help them
Don't join in with the killing
Are you willing to save them?
Don't kill, join in to save them
Please save them
Or one day they will never
Be seen again!

Tom Eyre (8)
St Wilfrid's Catholic Primary School, Sheffield

Rainforest Poem

Please help stop this devastation
It's affecting all of the nation
The screeching of animals
The crashing of trees
Who would stop this, would you please?
We are losing oxygen
If we don't stop this, it will turn into a mess
We need to stop this stress
Please help!

Joshua Fernandes (10)
St Wilfrid's Catholic Primary School, Sheffield

Save The World

I am writing to save the world and you should too
It won't just be good for the rainforest, it will be good for you
If you cut the trees down
And build and build a big large town
It takes a long time for a rainforest to grow
So don't do it, it's not an open show
So keep the rainforest, the animals might need a pear
And we need no polluted air
So will you walk to school and say I have saved trees today?

Alexandra Davidson (8)
St Wilfrid's Catholic Primary School, Sheffield

Littering

Save our wonderful planet from litter
Make it a better place
Put litter in the bin
Litter is filling seas
Don't just leave it there, pick it up
It can cause disease, it would be good
If you heard this message, not a lot of people would
And if you did, it would make this planet
Healthy and good.

Will Speechley (8)
St Wilfrid's Catholic Primary School, Sheffield

Polar Poem

Look out, the meltdown is about
What should we do? What should we do?

The polar region is shrinking because we're not really thinking
What should we do? What should we do?

We can use less fuel, maybe walk to school
Or use less lights to calm down the fright
The possibilities go on and on
So do one now before the ice is all gone!

Francesca Danks (8)
St Wilfrid's Catholic Primary School, Sheffield

Rainforest Destruction, Disaster

Why do you do this? It is not helping
How do you know it is going to be good?
You are not saving the animals or us.

Why can you not hear the animals shrieking?
Why? Why? Why? Why? Why?
The human race could be ending
The human race is a disgrace
Please listen to me.

William Allen (10)
St Wilfrid's Catholic Primary School, Sheffield

Be Green

Recycle a bit more because you can save the planet
Cycle or walk instead of driving sometimes because you can
You can do it, I know you can, so join in, come on
Why, oh why is the world not recycling much?
We have to do something quickly
Recycle, recycle, recycle is what we do
Everyone can recycle
Please help save the planet, please, please!

Siobhan Phillips (7)
St Wilfrid's Catholic Primary School, Sheffield

Be Green, Don't Be Mean

The world is a disgrace
Let's make it a better place
Big gaps in the rainforest
It ain't fair all the trees want is CO_2
Don't waste paper
it contributes to global warming
So recycle, save the rainforest
From reaching the forest floor.

Matthew Quarrell (9)
St Wilfrid's Catholic Primary School, Sheffield

Save The Rainforests

The rainforests are being chopped down
And the king is losing his crown
The animals are moving from home to home
And there are so many moans
Don't hurt or surround them
After all, you're on their ground.

Iona McKerrow (8)
St Wilfrid's Catholic Primary School, Sheffield

Don't Drop Litter

Don't drop litter
Litter will pollute
The planet will look dirty
Litter will smell
And hurt animals
Don't drop litter even in the winter
Don't throw it in the water
You will harm our planet.

William Gibson (7)
St Wilfrid's Catholic Primary School, Sheffield

Please, Please Stop!

Chopping trees down will ruin animals' habits
So please, please stop
Cutting trees down, it will just ruin nature
We wouldn't be able to breathe
And we will be the next one to die
We would have no animals to eat
We just wouldn't live that long
So please, please, stop cutting trees down.

Matilda Alleway (7)
St Wilfrid's Catholic Primary School, Sheffield

Get Rid Of Litter

Please don't drop litter on the street
Recycle it or put it in the bin
It does not even matter
If it is made of tin
No one likes a dirty world
So put it in the bin!

Zara Osako (7)
St Wilfrid's Catholic Primary School, Sheffield

The Rats

If you drop your litter
I have to pick it up
It really looks a mess
A can of Coke, a broken cup
Sweet wrappers, banana skins
They don't look very nice
I wish you would put it in the bin
Or we'll have lots of rats and mice.

Hope Hogan (7)
St Wilfrid's Catholic Primary School, Sheffield

Recycle

If no one recycled, if no one cared
The world would fill up with rubbish
So recycle your old plastic and glass
In the right place
Or use it again
To become an eco-kid
You have to reuse and recycle
Save our planet!

Grace Woods (8)
St Wilfrid's Catholic Primary School, Sheffield

Recycling And Litter

Save the Earth by recycling more
Don't drop litter
Dropping litter it is bad for the environment
If you stop recycling, you are not helping
If you recycle we will all free-cycle
Recycling is good for the world.

Olivia Murphy (9)
St Wilfrid's Catholic Primary School, Sheffield

Save The Polluted Seas

Save the fish, save the sea
It could harm you and me
Think of the pollution stirring as we swim
The sea helps the world not to be dim
What about the endangered animals dying as we speak?
The pollution is making the sea so bleak
So stop the pollution, stop it now
Don't say you don't know how.

Sam Keogh (10)
St Wilfrid's Catholic Primary School, Sheffield

Reduce, Reuse, Recycle

Keep recycling a little bit more
So come on and do it more
If you put recycling in
Then you get music out
So come on, come on now
Let's keep recycling
If you don't use something
Give it to someone else.

Sam Rodgers (8)
St Wilfrid's Catholic Primary School, Sheffield

Litter

If the world was full of litter
It would be so bad
If you don't put your litter in the bin
It would make everybody sad and mad
Don't throw your litter on the floor
Otherwise you'll be out the door.

Isabelle Cain (9)
St Wilfrid's Catholic Primary School, Sheffield

Save All The Rainforests

The rainforest is very bright
But sometimes you might get a fright
You will find lots of colourful frogs
But now you will not find many logs
You will find some shimmering rivers
But you will find lots of people that live
If we don't save the rainforests
All this will be gone!

Hannah Simpson (9)
St Wilfrid's Catholic Primary School, Sheffield

Bins

If you drop litter on the ground
There will be rats around
When you drop litter on the floor
Rats will spread all around
If you drop glass and litter on the beach
You could endanger sea creatures
If you drop litter, bugs will choke on the rubbish
Don't drop litter, put it in the bin instead!

Dmitri Cheetham (7)
St Wilfrid's Catholic Primary School, Sheffield

Don't Drop Litter

If there's bins around, then don't drop it on the ground
It will smell, it will not look nice
Animals are around, if they choke, they will die
It just will not be good
So you should not leave it on the ground.

Rachel Mathews (7)
St Wilfrid's Catholic Primary School, Sheffield

The Rainforest!

The big green trees rustling in the wind
Dark brown tree trunks swaying in the wind
The animals playing in the trees
The birds hunting for food
The frogs swimming on little leaves
Tigers playing and eating other animals in the tree
The rainforest is a place for animals
Not for cutting down trees.

Alex Middleton (8)
St Wilfrid's Catholic Primary School, Sheffield

The Beautiful Rainforests

Rainforests are beautiful places
Stretching for thousands of miles
Huge brown trees
Yellow and black bees
The multicoloured flowers
Their magic healing powers
So if they're cutting down trees
Say *no!*

Daniel O'Sullivan (8)
St Wilfrid's Catholic Primary School, Sheffield

Stop The War!

The war can kill people and children, also you!
Why do you pay money to fight because they defend themselves?
Why don't you agree about something instead of fighting?
They have to run on sand whilst they're fighting
Stop the war!

Francesca Shield (7)
St Wilfrid's Catholic Primary School, Sheffield

Rainforest Takeaway

The trees are getting cut down
From the ground, getting turned into paper that we don't need
We might all die, running out of oxygen supply
What we really need to survive
We will all die, I repeat we will all die
Then we will go very, very, very, very high in the sky
The only things left, the sea creatures will rule.

Alex Yeardley (7)
St Wilfrid's Catholic Primary School, Sheffield

Rainforest, Big Book Of Poetry

Don't be mean to green
Don't cut it down with machines
Don't destroy the animals' homes
You might injure some animals
Stop, before it's too late
Stop, stop, stop
Save the world!

Maeve O'Sullivan (8)
St Wilfrid's Catholic Primary School, Sheffield

Rainforest Devastation

The rainforest is getting killed
But you can help with nicer habitats we can build
The animals scream as the trees crash
As the machinery goes, the trees fall, there is a big bash
Waterfalls pour as the animals drink
So now it's up to you, you've just got to think
So come on and help us out.

Mhairi Marciniak (10)
St Wilfrid's Catholic Primary School, Sheffield

Stop Litter

Save our planet from horrible litter
Use the bins and don't drop litter
It can make a bad disease
The seas are filling up with litter
The fish are dying
The factories are making the air smell horrible
We hate litter!

Benjamin Walsh (7)
St Wilfrid's Catholic Primary School, Sheffield

Save The Rainforest

The Amazon rainforest is falling down
What will help . . .
Save the world, you can do it
Help the world by using recycled paper
Be an eco-warrior
Fight against the destroyers
Save the world, you can do it.

Harry Curtis (8)
St Wilfrid's Catholic Primary School, Sheffield

Don't Drop Litter!

Don't drop litter
It is wrong
It will smell
Glass will smash
Don't drop litter
It will attract
Mice.

Hannah Sharples (7)
St Wilfrid's Catholic Primary School, Sheffield

Pollution, Pollution

Pollution, pollution is ever so bad
Cars squirt smoke out, how awful is that?
Boats leave oil in the sea
The poor fish will die
Trains leave diesel, it affects the animals
Rabbits, squirrels and things like that all die
We've got to stop it or it will get worse.

Loretta Deeney (7)
St Wilfrid's Catholic Primary School, Sheffield

Stop Polluting The World

The government is not doing anything about the polluting
Nothing is happening, so what can you do?
Try recycling, it's good, it doesn't do anything wrong
If we made a solution, so we could stop polluting
We could make something what works
If you get this message, *remember*
Make the world happy!

James Foletti (8)
St Wilfrid's Catholic Primary School, Sheffield

The Rainforest

The rainforest was so big, beautiful and bright
But now all the animals in it are in terrible fright
All the animals were so happy, but have now left their homes
Now all they hear is just a load of phones
The whole world is greedy, now getting grey
And now we have to pay
So let's all turn it around and have a beautiful day.

Michael Smith (11) & Tom Uttley (10)
St Wilfrid's Catholic Primary School, Sheffield

Save Our Planet

The big green poetry machine is visiting to say
There are lots of things happening, so do it all today
Please don't cut down trees, it's killing all the bees.

So come on, save the universe, it's happening all today
Why stop and wait?
Be quick and do it before it's too late!

Bruce Gillespie (8)
St Wilfrid's Catholic Primary School, Sheffield

War World

Don't start wars, war affects the world
Don't destroy the Earth, make it grow old
Plants are dying because of bombs polluting the world
We've got to stop, people will die
Nobody will *save the world!*

Tim Pickin (7)
St Wilfrid's Catholic Primary School, Sheffield

Animals Matter

We love the animals
So can you keep them safe?
Keep the jungles safe for animals
Don't kill or cut them down
We love animals
So keep them right
Some love can help
Keep the world a safe place
Do we want a happy face?
Yes!

Shannon Lesley Byles (10)
Sacred Heart Primary School, Middlesbrough

Whales

Grey whales, humpback whales
Sea whales, minki whales
Those are my whales
They move gently
Swirling next to me
The strong, massive, blue whales
Have strong muscles in their tails
The large, extraordinary creatures
Have amazing little features
Sperm whales go down great depths in the sea
I hope they come back for a breath like you and me
The whales that live in lovely lagoons
Look as gorgeous as the moon
To stop the whales yelp, we all need to help
So use less oil, also kitchen foil
This is why whales are going to be in fairy tales
So don't forget, Orca whales, fin whales
Bottlenose whales, pygmy sperm whales
Save the whales.

Joeanna Appleby (9)
Sacred Heart Primary School, Middlesbrough

Save The Planet

Leave the animals that are old
Because if you don't they will get cold
They will have to go to the RSPCA
And you will be the one who will pay
Frogs, orang-utans, leopards and birds
Leave them alone
Otherwise you will be dead
They have done nothing to you
Only you're the one who knew.

Samera Rashad
Sacred Heart Primary School, Middlesbrough

Save The World

S ea life destroyed
A nimals distraught
V ery cautious about saving electricity
E co-friendly we must be

T he planet is wasting away
H elp the world, day by day
E nergy, we must save

W ind generators they are great
O rang-utans dying at a massive rate
R euse, recycle
L ittle things like the air cycle
D angerous gases pollute the world

Global warming is a global warning!

Chesley Conlin (10)
Sacred Heart Primary School, Middlesbrough

Untitled

Recycle, recycle
Save the world
Recycle, recycle
Save the mammals
If we don't the world will be polluted
Recycle, recycle
Keep us safe
Recycle, recycle
Save us all
If we do, we could make
The world a better place
So . . .
Recycle, recycle
Save the future.

Declan Marron
Sacred Heart Primary School, Middlesbrough

Keeping Animals Safe

Animals all around the world
They're not like any boy or girl
Their habitats are fading away day by day
Help the polar bears, brown bears too
This isn't just about me and you
Even if they are vicious, what have they done to you?
Even their lives, don't take them away
Fish are animals to think about
Fish on a dish, it's just not right
If you are going to save them
Save them with a smile, save them now!

Emily Craig
Sacred Heart Primary School, Middlesbrough

Animals Matter

We love animals
So keep them safe
Pumas help us so we can help them
Without orang-utans
We wouldn't be here
Keep the jungles
For the world
Because pumas and orang-utans matter
Without them no jungle will chatter.

Bethany Hurst
Sacred Heart Primary School, Middlesbrough

Green Issues

If you're young, old or teen
You can . . .
Save the animals
Help the world
Keep the place tidy
Help keep birds and other nature
Keep the jungle safe and sound
Do your bit.

Hannah Kay
Sacred Heart Primary School, Middlesbrough

Save The Planet

Help the animals
Save the jungle
Keep the rainforests
Neat and tidy
Don't be mean
Keep the green
Animals are waiting
For us to help.

Sophie Kendall (10)
Sacred Heart Primary School, Middlesbrough

Save The Environment

Turn off your lights
Do it now
Don't be cruel
Help school by saving
So start saving now
Not later, now.

Luke Henderson-Thynne (10)
Sacred Heart Primary School, Middlesbrough

Saving Water

Turn off the tap and do a good rap
Saving water
Saving money in a funny way
Go on, go green, then make a nice cuisine
Save electricity and be happy
Big or small you can crawl
Turn off the socket
You will save a rocket.

Matthew Hughes (10)
Sacred Heart Primary School, Middlesbrough

Save The World

Save the planet
Save the world
Leave the animals
Leave the trees
Leave the plants
Stop the tree cutting
Stop global warming
Leave the animals to be alone!

Dell Labonete (10)
Sacred Heart Primary School, Middlesbrough

Save The Planet

Save the world
Save trees
Save the animals
Save the people with no homes
Save the jungles in the world
Earth needs to be a safe place.

Georgia Gillespie
Sacred Heart Primary School, Middlesbrough

Save The World

Recycle, recycle, do it today
Recycle, recycle, every day

Save the tiger and destroy the lighter
Turn off the lights
Because the light is shining bright
Go to school and don't be a fool
Drive a car and don't go far.

Paulius Sivecas (10)
Sacred Heart Primary School, Middlesbrough

Eco Safe

E nvironment not safe for humans
C an we make a difference?
O f course we can

S o eco-warriors
A ll over the world
F ight for a better planet
E co-friendly we want to be.

Adam Loughran
Sacred Heart Primary School, Middlesbrough

Save The Green

Save the planet
Help the animals
Save the jungle
Don't destroy Earth
Save the green
Don't be mean
Don't destroy land.

Brad Gill
Sacred Heart Primary School, Middlesbrough

Saving The Planet

Turn off the light
Turn off the world
Don't matter if you're big or small
Then do us a favour
Reduce your carbon
Come on everybody
Let's give it a try.

Sara Atfi (11)
Sacred Heart Primary School, Middlesbrough

The Planet Poem

Help us save the world by recycling rubbish
The jungle needs us so come on, let's do it
You'll help us all and you'll have a ball
So come on, come on, come on, let's do it.

Paige Graham
Sacred Heart Primary School, Middlesbrough

Saving Our Planet

Remember, remember to recycle your paper
Do it now, don't do it later
Reuse your toilet rolls
You could make tall flagpoles
A box could be a home
When you're recycling
Please don't moan
You can reuse glass
We learnt this in our class
Earth is a disgrace
Help us to make it a better place.

James Harling (7)
Wrawby St Mary's CE Primary School, Wrawby

Remember, Remember To Recycle

Remember, remember to recycle your paper
Do it now, don't do it later
Recycle your toilet rolls
You may make them into flagpoles
Go round the streets picking up rubbish
Make it into something it is very fun
It's all in your memory
Make a great invention
Or take it to the recycling station
Make it out of boxes
Paint a picture of foxes
Remember, remember to reuse it
Make sure you just don't sit.

Abigail Lucy Laycock (7)
Wrawby St Mary's CE Primary School, Wrawby

Recycling, Recycling

Remember, remember to recycle your cardboard boxes of food
Or you'll get booed
Remember, remember to reuse your toilet rolls
You could make some flagpoles
Remember, remember to reuse your plastic bottles
You could make rocket bottles
Remember, remember to recycle your tins
Don't throw them in the bin
Remember, remember to reuse your boxes
They could make good foxes.

Sadie Rickell (7)
Wrawby St Mary's CE Primary School, Wrawby

Recycling

Remember, remember, to recycle your paper
You could make them into paper dancers
Remember, remember to recycle your toilet rolls
You could make them into flagpoles
Take your waste to the recycling centre
And make sure you put it in the right bins
Recycle your clear glass and brown glass
We want this in our class
Recycle your paper don't do it later.

Caitlin Almond (8)
Wrawby St Mary's CE Primary School, Wrawby

Recycling

Remember, remember to recycle your paper
Do it now, don't do it later
Put your boxes in the recycling bin with your tomato tins
Remember, remember to recycle your toilet rolls
To make telescopes and flagpoles
Remember, remember to recycle your tins
And take them to recycling bins
Put your washing up bottles in the bin
To make a model person with a chin.

Kizzie Platt (8)
Wrawby St Mary's CE Primary School, Wrawby

Recycling

Remember, remember to recycle tins
Remember, remember to take your boxes to the recycling bin
Remember, remember to reuse your toilet rolls
You could use them for football goals.

Joshua Watson (7)
Wrawby St Mary's CE Primary School, Wrawby

Recycling

Remember, remember to recycle your boxes
So they can be turned into Oxo boxes
Remember to recycle your soup tins
You could make them into bins
Remember, remember recycle your paper
Do it now, don't do it later
Remember recycle your toilet rolls
And they can be turned into flagpoles.

Samuel Lewis (8)
Wrawby St Mary's CE Primary School, Wrawby

Recycle

Remember, remember to recycle every day
Don't do it in the morning
Remember, remember to recycle toilet rolls
So they can be reused
Remember, remember to throw out vegetable peelings
Do it now
Remember, remember to recycle bottles and cans
Make sure that you don't miss the dustbin lorry.

Steven Smith (8)
Wrawby St Mary's CE Primary School, Wrawby

Recycling

Remember, remember to recycle paper
Do it now, don't do it later
Remember, remember to recycle boxes
To help pretty foxes
Remember, remember to reuse toilet rolls
You could use them as flagpoles.

Edward White (7)
Wrawby St Mary's CE Primary School, Wrawby

Saving Our Planet

Remember, remember to recycle your cans
They could come back as sparkling pans
Remember, remember to recycle your paper
Do it now, don't do it later
Remember, remember to recycle your veg
Don't just leave it on the ledge
Remember, remember to recycle your litter
And then you might get fitter.

Charlie Reynolds
Wrawby St Mary's CE Primary School, Wrawby

Recycle Your Things

Remember to recycle your paper
Always do it not, not later
Always remember to recycle your toilet rolls
Don't let them drop into holes
Remember, remember to recycle your bottles
That are plastic
Do not let something go that is elastic.

Tristan Miller (7)
Wrawby St Mary's CE Primary School, Wrawby

Recycling

Remember, remember to recycle your paper
Do it now, don't do it later
Remember, remember to recycle your plastic
And don't throw out any elastic
Remember, remember to recycle cardboard boxes
And you will save the homes of foxes.

Janey Smith (8)
Wrawby St Mary's CE Primary School, Wrawby

Recycling

Remember to recycle cardboard boxes
You could turn them into model foxes
Remember to recycle toilet rolls
To make them into football goals
Remember to recycle glass
We learnt this in our class.

Ross Tandon (7)
Wrawby St Mary's CE Primary School, Wrawby

Recycling

Remember, remember to recycle your boxes
Make them into model foxes
Remember, remember to recycle paper
To make you a person that is greater
Remember, remember to recycle your plastic
Do it now, don't do it later.

Nicole Barnard (9)
Wrawby St Mary's CE Primary School, Wrawby

Young Writers Information

We hope you have enjoyed reading this book - and that you will continue to enjoy it in the coming years.

If you like reading and writing poetry drop us a line, or give us a call, and we'll send you a free information pack.

Alternatively if you would like to order further copies of this book or any of our other titles, then please give us a call or log onto our website at www.youngwriters.co.uk

Young Writers Information
Remus House
Coltsfoot Drive
Peterborough
PE2 9JX
(01733) 890066